The Bruce Lee Library
Volume 1

Interviews 1958–1973

Words of the Dragon

Edited by **John Little**

Charles E. Tuttle Co., Inc.
Boston Rutland, Vermont Tokyo

First published in 1997 by Tuttle Publishing, an imprint of Periplus Editions (HK) Ltd., with editorial offices at 153 Milk Street, Boston, Massachusetts 02109.

Library of Congress Catalog Card Number: 97-61947

Distributed by

USA
Charles E. Tuttle Co., Inc.
RR 1 Box 231-5
North Clarendon, VT 05759
Tel.: (802) 773-8930
Fax.: (802) 773-6993

Japan
Tuttle Shokai Ltd.
1-21-13, Seki
Tama-ku, Kawasaki-shi
Kanagawa-ken 214, Japan
Tel.: (044) 833-0225
Fax.: (044) 822-0413

Southeast Asia
Berkeley Books Pte. Ltd.
5 Little Road #08-01
Singapore 536983
Tel.: (65) 280-3320
Fax.: (65) 280-6290

First edition
05 04 03 02 01   00 99 98 97   1 3 5 7 9 10 8 6 4 2

Text and cover design—Vernon Press, Inc.

Printed in the United States of America

To the fans and friends of Bruce Lee—
of every race, color, and creed.

Not only have you appreciated and understood
the message that Bruce Lee delivered
through his films and writings,
but your sincere and on-going support
has insured that the flame of his work
has continued to burn brightly
for well over two decades.

It is you who have made
the significance of its illumination
known to all.

CONTENTS

Part 3: The Hollywood Years (1967–1970)

Part 4: The Hong Kong Years (1971–1973)

ACKNOWLEDGMENTS

No one person could bring together such a collection of articles without assistance. First and foremost, I owe a debt of gratitude to Linda Lee Cadwell, Bruce's wife from 1964 to 1973, for having the pride and disposition to clip and save the various interviews and articles that were written about her husband (particularly those from the early 1960s).

My appreciation also extends to Adrian Marshall, Bruce Lee's lawyer from 1969 until Lee's passing in 1973. Both Linda and Adrian have given me solid encouragement in all of the numerous Bruce Lee–related projects I'm involved with.

Many of the publications from which I've excerpted materials are now defunct. In all cases, however, an attempt was made to locate either the authors or publishers of these materials for permission to reprint them. Where I was successful, the articles and interviews have been tagged "Reprinted with permission." Where it proved impossible, I've provided those elements of the credits (publication, author, date, etc.) to which I had access.

Nevertheless, I owe a huge debt of gratitude to the men and women who wrote these articles for their work in preserving a unique aspect of martial arts heritage. I would also like to thank the following publications for permission to reprint the selections in this volume of the Bruce Lee Library:

Associated Press
Chicago's American
China Mail (Hong Kong)
Gastonia Gazette
Hong Kong Standard
Little-Wolff Creative Group
Miami Beach Sun
Miami News (Florida Report)
Movie Mirror
New Nation (Singapore)
Off Duty/Pacific
Seattle Post-Intelligencer
Seattle Times

St. Paul Pioneer Press
Sunday Post Herald (Hong Kong)
The Star (Hong Kong)
The Tribune
TV and Movie Screen
TV Picture Life
TV Radio Mirror
TV Radio Show
United Press International
Washington Daily News
Washington Post
Washington Star

—John Little

PREFACE

Editor's note: I had intended to have Linda Lee Cadwell write a short preface that would explain the significance of her late husband and his work as well as the enduring impact he has had on the worlds of film, martial art, physical fitness, athletics, and philosophy. Above all, I had hoped she would share with the reader her views of the man behind the legendary figure.

But I happened upon a brief article in a Hong Kong magazine that Linda wrote for release in conjunction with Bruce Lee's third film, *The Way of the Dragon*, in December 1972. The article is entitled "Do You Know Bruce Lee?" and it strikes me as poignant and informative and, moreover, exactly what I was looking for to preface this book. In addition, when considered in conjunction with the "last word" article about Bruce Lee at the end of the book, which was written at approximately the same time by eight-year-old Brandon Lee, it serves as an apt frame for the book. Linda has graciously consented to its being reprinted here.

As this book is about coming to understand Bruce Lee and his life as seen through the eyes of the press, Linda and Brandon's respective articles offer insights born of warm, personal experiences with Bruce Lee that nicely offset the often cold, impersonal reporting of journalists. In addition, Linda's and Brandon's insights reveal to us just how dedicated Bruce Lee was to the noble task of producing work of quality and substance, which is why his name and work have withstood the test of time and will continue to endure into the future, inspiring new generations of dedicated artists in all walks of life.

—John Little

DO YOU KNOW BRUCE LEE?

Do you know Bruce Lee? If I had said "Do you know who Bruce Lee is?" almost every man, woman, and child in Hong Kong and Southeast Asia, and many people in the rest of the world would immediately answer: "Yes! Bruce Lee is a movie actor who has lots of money, a big house, beautiful cars, who is strikingly handsome, and can physically perform feats which astonish and thrill movie goers time and time again." But do you really know Bruce Lee? I have been married to him for nearly nine years, been closer to him than any other human being during that time, and still I have to say, I don't know Bruce Lee completely. But perhaps I know him better than most, and I would like to shed some light on this question—Who Is Bruce Lee? When I first decided to write this article about my husband, I thought how complicated it would be to write about him in a few lines, but I then realized that this is actually a simple task because Bruce Lee is a simple man. He is a simple man because he simply knows what he wants and he directly and honestly goes about achieving it. He does not take detours, or make compromises, or go the easy way; he does not play games with people like being nice to the right ones and stepping on others; he is not tempted by fantastic deals, offers of money or fame, or promises of security: He simply knows what he wants and with a great deal of care he goes about achieving it. This is because Bruce Lee knows himself and this has not been a simple task. It didn't happen overnight, it has been a process of many years. It is a process which continues every day of his life. This is why I can never say that I know all about this man because he is constantly growing, discovering, changing, expanding his horizons. It is an exciting process and he is an extremely exciting person to live with. I would like to tell you how Bruce, at least in the ten years that I've known him, has evolved to the man he is today while still being the same man I married years ago. As objectively as possible I will talk about Bruce so you will also know him better and appreciate him, as I do, as an extraordinary human being.

When I first met Bruce we were both college students. We had a lot of fun, few worries, and didn't think much about the future. He taught a small group of aspiring martial artists, and this was exotic and appealing to those who flocked around Bruce. As our relationship developed and those thoughts of the future became more prominent, we decided to get married. I couldn't have known then that it was to be the best and most important thing that ever happened to me. I couldn't have known at that moment of the richness of life I have been privileged to share since that time. For Bruce, the acquisition of a wife and a year later a son, brought added responsibilities and all at once his life did seem complicated. The ordinary thing to do was get a job, thereby acquiring security, provide for his family, and exist. But even then, Bruce was never content with just existing—he had something else: his dreams! He didn't know then, but his dreams were beginning to contain shades of reality; his instinctive far-sightedness was beginning to have more influence on his future. Through those years when he was not rich, but happy, he studied extensively, he practiced his martial art intensely, he dreamed, and his goals became clearer. His complicated life was becoming simpler.

After the days of "The Green Hornet" TV series, with a small taste of wealth, and a well-publicized reputation as a capable martial artist, it would have been easy to strike while the iron was hot and establish a nationwide chain of gung fu schools. Oriental martial arts in the United States are big business and that would have been an easy money-maker and resulted in a life of luxury for Bruce. But by then, he knew what he wanted, his dreams had become definite goals, and a chain of martial art schools wasn't in the plan. Friends and relatives urged him do it, to grab this opportunity, but Bruce has never been one to grab opportunities, instead he makes his own opportunities. His years of practicing had developed an intense care for martial art and he couldn't sacrifice his art to the masses where he wouldn't have control of the quality. This word *quality* expresses a great deal about Bruce—whatever he does, be it a small action or a large decision, reflects quality.

The next six years were not easy ones, often depressing and discouraging, sometimes a feast, more often a famine. But the goal was set, there was no going back although at any time it would have been easy to cash in on his martial art fame. He has the strength of his convictions (which many have) but also the courage to carry them out (a rare quality). Even during those years when there seemed to be no reward for his efforts, he drove himself hard, subjected himself to constant self-improvement. He wasn't content to scratch the surface of his ambition, he dug deep into his fields—training daily, studying the physical body and every kind of combat: Western, Eastern, ancient, modern; delving into the philosophies of men of various beliefs: oriental and occidental; examining the ways of filmmakers around the world; and in all, retaining the appropriate and rejecting the unsuitable. This instinctive good judgment allowed him to learn and retain something from every situation, whether a meeting with a famous American actor or passing the time with a waiter in a restaurant. He took notes of his thoughts, wrote reminders of encouragement to himself, kept his thinking positive. He hung a sign on the wall which said "Walk On!" and he did just that. He overcame his bad times because he has the ability to endure and knows that, to be a success, he has to put in a lot of hard work.

But Bruce could not just be a thinker—he had to be a doer. And he saw his opportunity. In the States, he had seen many recent Chinese movies. He knew they could be better and be saw himself as the one to do it. And so there came *The Big Boss* and *Fist of Fury,* which are already history. His constant desire to better himself has now produced *The Way of the Dragon,* which he undertook to direct himself, as well as writing the screenplay, and acting the lead. With tremendous dedication and the energy of ten, he patiently and painstakingly applied himself to every detail of the film, directing his attention to every department from set decoration to dubbing the sound, and from choosing the appropriate music to even playing one of the musical instruments in the background. And the results are worthy of his efforts. The first time I saw *The Way of the Dragon,* I was amazed that he had the talents and imagination to produce this quality of film, especially on his first directorial attempt. And so rich are his inner resources that there will only be better things to come. By making better and better films, he seeks not to be more famous or more wealthy, but to be appreciated and to heighten the appreciation of the audience.

I think it has been Bruce's destiny to become a filmmaker because he has the ability to honestly observe humanity and to truthfully express it on the screen—together with the rare quality called charisma, which is difficult to translate into Chinese and equally difficult to explain in English. But I would say charisma is a force of concentration which flows from the screen to the audience; an immediate warm, personal relationship with the character; a strength of personality which triggers instant appeal; and over all, an intense grace. Bruce has constant awareness of emotions around him and within himself. He is every minute of every day discovering new things, adding the essential, hacking away the unessential, forever growing and expanding.

Yes, Bruce is a success—he has willed his dreams to reality. He could now cease his constant striving. He could easily make twenty films in rapid succession, or sign a ten-million-dollar contract, and take it easy. But he never will. He will put his heart and soul into each film searching for a better way to show man to himself through the medium of entertainment. You may see only one or two Bruce Lee films a year, but you will remember them.

How long can he continue to use these enormous amounts of energy? How far can he expand? I see no limit. From my close relationship with him over the years and my knowledge of how he works, I believe that Bruce will make a giant contribution to film-making and find a special place in the hearts and minds of generations to come. He has only just begun!

—Linda Lee Cadwell

Introduction

In 1994, Linda Lee Cadwell, the widow of Bruce Lee, paid me the tremendous and unprecedented honor of being the first person she ever allowed to go through every scrap of her late husband's personal papers, notes, letters, essays, rough drafts of screenplays, choreography notes, poetry, art work, reading annotations, and daytime diaries in an attempt to put together a multivolume testament to his incredible legacy and reveal the human being behind the legendary persona.

During the course of conducting this research I happened upon a scrapbook that Linda had kept since she first started dating Bruce Lee. It was fascinating inasmuch as it contained a chronological evolution of Bruce's thoughts, life, career, and martial art. It struck me then that the newspapers and magazines that had had the foresight to interview this young man were, in effect, recording a very significant piece of history for martial artists around the world: the documented history of one of the most electrifying and dedicated thinkers of the twentieth century, Bruce Lee.

Those who think of Bruce Lee simply as a "karate guy," will learn just how far off base such an assumption is. You're about to discover the many dimensions of the man. Through the pages of this book you will be given the opportunity to meet Bruce Lee the philosopher, the joker, the husband, the father. You will meet a dedicated martial artist and filmmaker who was determined to free his associates in both fields from the shackles of their own ignorance and their craven fear of change. You'll also meet a man who faced almost permanent prejudice in being Chinese—not only from producers (for example, William Dozier's insulting method of informing Bruce that "The Green Hornet" TV series was canceled; see "Kato Likes Puns, Preys on Words," pages 80–82) but from those in the media who really had no excuse for such ignorance and cruelty.

You will also come to learn how dealing with stereotypical images of his culture was the type of thing Bruce Lee endured on an almost daily basis—particularly in his early years in the United States—and an obstacle that he resolved to overcome. Lee would ultimately succeed through the application of his indomitable will and a highly cultivated talent. The comments of his critics would, in time, fade into oblivion. In contrast, Lee's words and ideas are still repeated, almost with an air of religious sanctity and piety, some two decades after his passing, inspiring all of us who were fortunate enough to read them to "walk on."

I believe that this book provides a means to understand Bruce Lee as never before—the real Bruce Lee, that is, as opposed to the movie star you may have encountered on the big screen or on your VCR. You'll be by his side through his career transitions: from childhood actor to university student; from dedicated gung fu practitioner to maverick martial arts pioneer. You'll witness his acting career evolution; from Kato on TV's "The Green Hornet," through bit parts in MGM's *Marlowe*, to the international superstar he became in films such as *The Big Boss*, *Fist of Fury*, *The Way of the Dragon*, and *Enter the Dragon*.

Beyond the trappings of celebrity, however, you'll meet a real human being. Of particular poignancy is Fredda Dudley Balling's interview with Bruce Lee for *TV and Movie Screen*, a now-defunct Hollywood publication that thrived in the mid 1960s (see "Bruce Lee: Love Knows No Geography," pages 35–42). In this interview, Bruce Lee opened up about his plans to raise his then newborn son, Brandon, and how he didn't view Brandon as being the unfortunate victim of an interracial marriage but, on the contrary, the beneficiary of the best of two cultures, East and West.

It was this desire to educate the West in the ways of the East and to educate the East in the ways of the West that marked a great deal of Bruce Lee's life. In his early years, he was delighted to have the opportunity to share his Chinese heritage and its rich culture with the Western media. Shortly before his death, his emphasis was on raising the standard of the then-primitive ways of Eastern film production, along with their story lines, in hope that one day Chinese films would be taken seriously in the international market. While this did not happen during Lee's lifetime, it must be recognized that it was largely through his pioneering efforts in this regard that this eventually came to pass.

For the great majority, these articles and interviews represent never-before-heard wisdom, delivered firsthand by Bruce Lee himself. This book demands to be read and reread, and the words contained herein carefully weighed and considered. Amidst the puns and self-deprecating humor lies Bruce Lee's very real message of the absolute necessity of honest self-expression. That, in essence, was Lee's philosophy, not only of martial art but of life itself. Lee believed and attempted to convey to all who would listen that the individual represented the whole of mankind, and that the happiness, the knowledge, and the meaning that we each long for and seek from so many divergent sources ultimately resides within us all. His message is as pertinent today as it was at the time when the journalists he spoke with first jotted down his words for the articles and interviews you are about to read.

This is history's biography of Bruce Lee—with writers and journalists from all points of the compass playing Boswell to his Samuel Johnson.

It is his story—his message—in his own words; words that are pure, honest and, perhaps most importantly, untainted by any one biographer's opinion or filter of recollection. This is not to say that these journalists were above employing literary license with aspects of Lee's history. Nor were they sufficiently versed in martial arts nomenclature to differentiate between karate (a Japanese martial art) and gung fu (a Cantonese term that denotes excellence or total mastery in virtually any field of endeavor or profession, but that more popularly is utilized as a synonym for Chinese martial art). Nevertheless, despite the odd lapse of journalistic integrity— the notes at the end of each of the four parts of this book provide clarification of some of the more blatant transgressions in this regard—these interviews, taken together, form a unique story of talent, determination, and honesty triumphing over cant, second-hand artistry, and insincerity. And, in today's world, that's a story that needs to be told again and again.

—John Little

A Chronological List of Bruce Lee's Principal Works

Hong Kong

Bruce Lee made over twenty films during his childhood. His first (at the tender age of three months) was shot in San Francisco and entitled *Golden Gate Girl*. His last childhood film, *The Orphan*, was shot in Hong Kong in 1958. Other films included:

1946:   *The Birth of Mankind*
1950:   *Kid Cheung*
1953:   *It's Father's Fault*
        Myriad Homes
        A Mother's Tears
        In the Face of Demolition
1955:   *Orphan's Song*
        We Owe It to Our Children
        Love
1956:   *Too Late for Divorce*
1957:   *The Thunderstorm*

Hollywood

Television:

1966:   "The Green Hornet." Twentieth Century-Fox. Starring
        Van Williams and Bruce Lee.
        Bruce Lee filmed 26 episodes, which aired weekly on Friday from
        7:30–8:00 PM on the ABC television network.

1967:   "Batman." Twentieth Century-Fox. Starring Adam West and
        Burt Ward.
        Bruce Lee appeared as Kato in a special two-part episode of the
        popular ABC-TV series.

"Ironside."
Bruce Lee appears as a martial arts instructor who provides a clue to help solve a case.

1968: "Blondie."
Bruce Lee plays a martial arts instructor who trains the star of the show to help him to deal with a bully.

"Here Come the Brides."
Bruce Lee in a non-martial arts capacity, playing a young Chinese groom. The episode is entitled "Marriage, Chinese Style."

1971: "Longstreet." Paramount. Starring James Franciscus.
Bruce Lee appears in four episodes of the series, the first of which he co-wrote with his student Stirling Silliphant. The episode is entitled "The Way of the Intercepting Fist," the English translation of Lee's martial art of jeet kune do. The three additional episodes were entitled "Spell Legacy of Death," "Wednesday's Child," and "I See, Said the Blind Man."

"Bruce Lee: The Lost Interview."
Bruce Lee's only surviving video interview. Lee is interviewed in Hong Kong's TVB studios by Canadian broadcaster/author Pierre Berton. Airing only one time (in Canada in January 1972), as "The Pierre Berton Show with Bruce Li: Mandarin Superstar," it has since become known as "The Lost Interview," since it was believed to have been destroyed until it was located by Little-Wolff Creative Group in the Canadian Archives in 1994.

Films:

1968: *Marlowe*. MGM. Starring James Garner and Rita Moreno.
Bruce Lee plays a Chinese thug named Winslow Wong.

Fight Choreographer:

1968: *The Wrecking Crew*. Columbia Pictures. Starring Dean Martin, Sharon Tate, and Elke Sommer.
Bruce Lee was technical director in this movie that starred Dean Martin as special agent Matt Helm.

1969: *A Walk in the Spring Rain*. Columbia Pictures. Starring Anthony Quinn and Ingrid Bergman.
Bruce Lee was technical director for a fight scene that took place at the climax of the film.

Hong Kong

Films

1971: *The Big Boss* (North American title: *Fists of Fury*). Golden Harvest. Starring Bruce Lee, Maria Yi, James Tien, and Han Ying Chieh. Bruce Lee's first starring role firmly established him as an electrifying movie presence, smashing the all-time box office record set in Hong Kong (by *The Sound of Music*).

Fist of Fury (North American title: *The Chinese Connection*). Golden Harvest. Starring Bruce Lee, Nora Miao, James Tien, Bob Baker, and Lo Wei.
Obliterated the record set by *The Big Boss* and established Bruce Lee as a national hero.

1972: *The Way of the Dragon* (alternate title: *Return of the Dragon*). Concord. Starring Bruce Lee, Chuck Norris, Bob Wall, Nora Miao, and Jon T. Benn.
After the phenomenal success of his first two films for Golden Harvest, Bruce Lee formed his own production company, Concord Productions, with Golden Harvest founder, Raymond Chow. This film also set a new box-office record in Hong Kong.

The Game of Death. Unfinished.[1]

1973: *Enter the Dragon.* Warner Brothers. Starring Bruce Lee, John Saxon, Jim Kelly, Ahna Capri, Bob Wall, Shih Kien, Angela Mao, Yung Sze, Betty Chung, Geoffrey Weeks, and Peter Archer.
The high-water mark of all martial arts films, *Enter the Dragon*—and Bruce Lee's performance in it—have set it apart from every other martial arts movie ever made. The best of the genre.

Note

1. In 1972 Bruce Lee began preliminary filming for a philosophical/martial arts film called *The Game of Death*. However, his involvement in the production was interrupted to permit him to begin filming his next picture—Warner Brothers' *Enter the Dragon*. Lee had intended to resume work on *The Game of Death* in November 1973, but sadly did not live to return to the production. In fall 1978, Golden Harvest completely rewrote the film. Ignoring Lee's original intentions, it was completed with a stand-in and, at times, a cardboard cutout of Bruce Lee. It cannot be considered in any way a "Bruce Lee film" due to the almost complete lack of Lee's presence in the production and, indeed, in the film itself. (Lee only appears on screen for a total of twelve minutes.)

Part 1

THE
SEATTLE
YEARS

(1958–1964)

A BUDDING STAR OF CHINESE MOVIES

by Frank Lynch

HEY LOUELLA! You be interested in a young star from the Hollywood of the Far East? Lee Shiu Loong[1]*—Bruce Lee in the U. S. of A.—is a student at Edison. A protege of Ping Chow,[2] the noted restaurateur (Broadway and Jefferson). He is 18, born in San Francisco, taken to Hong Kong when he was three months of age.

His father, Lee Hoi Chuen, was a star of the ancient Chinese opera. Perhaps that background is what tipped the scales for Lee when they were looking for a six-year-old to play the lead in a moom picture called *The Beginning of a Boy*.

Lee's screen father was an honest, hard-working clerk. His screen mother flighty—in addition to that she gambled away the family's savings at mah-jong.

The screen Lee was a bit on the precocious side. Always the nose in the comic book. We are going to assume that the Chinese comic book is a notch or two above the ones favored by our grandchildren for Lee was fascinated by this particular story:

Far, far away there stood a mountain. A bandit gang or two lurking along the way and maybe the odd hungry tiger. The road to the top was steep and strewn with boulders. Yet he who reached the top would come down with the strength of ten. So the six-year-old set out for the mountain, eluded the bandits, and escaped the tigers and arrived, cold, hungry and afraid, at a monastery half-way to the summit. The monks took him in, fed him, let him warm himself at their fires and set him to chopping wood and running errands and things like that.

---

*Notes to Part 1 begin on page 28.

In some vague way the screen Lee knew that if he kept at same he would become strong and wise and maybe rich. Only it would take a long, long time. He fled down the mountain. Returned to his home city. Joined up with some no-goodnicks and became a pickpocket. Came the day he lifted a sucker's poke as per usual. Victim looked at thief and thief at victim. There was mutual recognition. Father started chasing son down the street. Son took off on a crossing against the red. Into the path of an impatient motorist. Oh, too bad, too bad.

Mother and father were shown, then, over the bed of the dying boy. The father said if he had worked harder, and put his son in a good school, it might not have happened at all. The mother said no, that it was all her fault. That she was away at mah-jong when she should have been teaching her son right from wrong. That when she lost she took her temper out on him and that is why he ran away. With that,

Stills from the Cantonese-language film The Orphan, *in which Bruce Lee had his first starring role, at age seventeen. Before this film, Lee had appeared only in co-starring or supporting roles.*

the screen Lee died. Everybody in the audience cried—then hurried out to tell everybody else what a hell of a picture it was.

In his second picture Lee portrayed a doorstep baby. Ignored by his wealthy father—abandoned by his serving-girl mother. Taken in by a gambler. Sold into servitude. To escape—to find a noble benefactor. The end of this finds Lee—played by an adult, of course, a celebrated doctor. He operates on the sweetheart of his youth and restores her sight even as he promised. His real father and his several foster fathers fawn upon him. He ignores them. The people who saw this bawled and cheered.

Lee's latest picture—made last spring and to be released presently—is known as *The Orphan*. It is a sort of blackboard jungle thing. Based on the activities of Hong Kong's two main juvenile gangs, the 14Ks and the Wo Sing Wo. (There is a moll gang too—the 18 Sisters).

The Orphan (Lee) is separated from father, mother and sister with the Japanese invasion. He survives the flying lead, bombings, hunger and disease to grow up to be a pickpocket too. A high-thinking man befriends him. The Orphan spurns his offers of aid. Continues to spurn them until he makes the bucket and is given this choice—school or seven years.

His pals talk him into one last caper. A snatch. He cops out from his pals and they, in turn, remove his ears from his noggin. We shall leave him earless and purified to tell you that just before he left he was named the cha-cha champ of all Hong Kong. That if the people at Edison can teach him some git-tar to go with the dancing he might reach the top of the real-life mountain. A couple of million bucks instead of the strength of ten but what's the dif?

Seattle Times[3]

MIKE LEE HOPE FOR ROTSA RUCK[4]

U Introduced to Gung Fu

by Weldon Johnson

At first Gung Fu sounds like a variety of Chow Mein. And after you think about it, you're pretty sure it is—but it really isn't.

Gung Fu is the Chinese art of pugilism, the oldest of all hand-to-hand combat. And because it has been shrouded under a veil of secrecy and reverence, Gung Fu is almost unknown outside China.

A guy who knows quite a bit about it walked into the office the other day. His name is Bruce Lee, from Hong Kong, and he's the youngest person ever to achieve Chinese rating in the art. "Gung Fu is prac-

Gung Fu is not preoccupied with breaking bricks and smashing boards, such as Karate. We're more concerned with having it affect our whole way of thinking and behaving.

ticed not only for health and self-protection, but for cultivation of the mind as well," Lee said.

Lee, a university student, and Fred Sato, judo expert, are currently appearing on KUOW Television's The Oriental Art of Self-Defense series. They will appear next Monday evening and the following Monday for a half hour, beginning at 7:00 PM.

"Gung Fu was used by Taoist priests and Chinese monks as a philosophy, or way of thinking, in which the ideals of giving with adversity, to bend slightly and then spring up stronger than before, are practiced," Lee said.

Lee said that the qualities of patience and profiting by one's mistakes are a part of the Gung Fu discipline. "There are two schools of Gung Fu," Lee said. "One is the 'hard school' which concentrates on speed, coordination, and physical power, like cracking bricks and stones with bare hands. The other school, the 'soft school' advocates gentleness and unity of mind and body—firmness is concealed in softness."

But Lee is quick to correct any misunderstanding about his art. "Gung Fu is not preoccupied with breaking bricks and smashing boards, such as Karate," he said. "We're more concerned with having it affect our whole way of thinking and behaving."

"The American is like an Oak Tree—he stands firm against the wind. If the wind is strong, he cracks," he said. "The Oriental stands like bamboo, bending with the wind and springing back when the wind ceases—stronger than ever before."

Lee is an unusual man. He's rather small, but walks with a spring, and can rip you into a Niagara of blood at the drop of a fortune cookie. "My strength comes from the abdomen," he said. "It's the center of gravity and the source of real power. One must learn to react, rather than plan his movements."

Lee recently held a demonstration with some of his student's physical education staff in the Pavilion. He said the Pavilion staff expressed "much interest," and he's hoping his series on KUOW will spark a flame of interest on campus. "If Gung Fu is adopted and taught in the Physical Education classes, it will be the first Gung Fu instruction in a university in the western world," Lee said.

That would make Lee, Gung Fu and Chow Mein manufacturers velly happy.

Seattle high school newspaper

BRUCE LEE, CHINESE MOVIE STAR, SPEAKS TO GARFIELD SENIORS

Gung Fu Is Way of Life as Well as Mode of Self-Defense, Lee Says

by Cindy Thal

Bruce Lee, 22 year old Chinese movie star, artist, Gung Fu master, and "Cha Cha King of Hong Kong," spoke recently at Garfield to a fascinated audience of seniors.

Although born in San Francisco, Bruce returned to China at the age of three months and received his education there.[5] "Hong Kong is really nice," he said, "I plan to go back in March."

Mixture of Ancient China–Modern America

A psychology major at the University of Washington, Bruce thinks of himself as an Americanized Chinese.[6] Five feet, seven inches tall and 140 pounds, Bruce learned British English and the techniques of Gung Fu.

Gung Fu Changes Life

"I began learning Gung Fu at 13 because I wanted to learn how to fight. Now it has changed my whole life and I have a completely different way of thinking." Taught by a Chinese master, the leader of the Wing Chun School of Gung Fu, Bruce, in five years became eligible as an instructor.[7]

Bruce Lee poses for a picture by The Columns on the campus of the University of Washington, where he was majoring in philosophy. (It was at this site where Lee first asked his future wife, Linda Emery, for a date.) Philosophy and its application to martial art and life (and later, to film) would remain Lee's passion.

"I want to establish Gung Fu institutes throughout the United States and write books about it," said Bruce about his future plans. "Gung Fu is a way of life as well as a mode of self defense. It is based on Yin (negative) and Yang (positive) where everything is a complement. Examples are softness with firmness, night with day and man with woman. It is a quiet awareness of one's opponent's strength and plans, and how to complement them."

Seattle newspaper, ca. 1961

GUNG FU DEMONSTRATION

On Monday, fans of the Oriental methods of self-defense will have an opportunity to see a demonstration of the granddaddy of them all—Gung Fu.

According to Bruce Lee, who will be giving the demonstration, Gung Fu is the world's oldest system of hand-to-hand combat.

It originated in China about 4,000 years ago.

Lee, who is a university sophomore, came into the DAILY newsroom a couple of days ago and gave us a private demonstration. It was quite enlightening.

Lee contends that Gung Fu, when done properly, is similar to complex dance. We agree. Some of the contortions he went through could put the twist in the shade easily. And if one were on the receiving end of the kicks and jabs, the damage might even be worse than the twist could inflict.

Lee was born in San Francisco, but moved to China when he was about three months old. He lived in Canton and Hong Kong.[8] He's been a student of Gung Fu for eight years

He believes Gung Fu, which is based on the philosophies of Taoism and Zen, is one of the most useful and hygienic activities he's discovered. Lee considers calisthenics and the like a waste of time and energy. Bruce didn't say whether he included the twist in the calisthenics category.

At any rate, Lee's demonstration will be the first and only one of its kind to take place in the area. The time is 3:30 PM, the place Meany Hall.

Notes

1. The correct phonetic spelling of Lee's Chinese name is Lee Siu Lung, "Lee Little Dragon." Bruce Lee was known by that name in Hong Kong throughout both his childhood and adult film careers. (It is interesting to note that Lee was born between 6:00 and 8:00 AM—in the Chinese Hour of the Dragon—on November 27, 1940, the Year of the Dragon.)
2. Bruce Lee was nobody's protégé, particularly not Ping Chow's. However, Lee did work for Chow as a busboy for a time after he first arrived in Seattle.
3. Reprinted with permission from the *Seattle Times.*
4. For unexplained reasons, the author mistakenly refers to Bruce Lee as "Mike Lee." Also surprising—if not altogether insulting—is the use of stereotype phonetics throughout the article.
5. Bruce Lee "returned" to Hong Kong (not China) and he received his grade-school education in Hong Kong.
6. Lee's major at the University of Washington was philosophy, not psychology.

7. Bruce Lee's teacher in this art was Yip Man, an elderly Chinese man. In his "Gung Fu Scrapbook," Lee wrote:

> The last master of the Wing Chun school was Professor Yip, born in Fut San in Southern China. Professor Yip started a study of the various schools of Gung fu at the age of 8, till he met Professor Chan Wa Shun, and immediately devoted his full energies to his art, the Wing Chun school. Now he is the present leader of that school. Professor Yip is truly a gung fu great, and is respected by other instructors of various schools. He is famous for his "sticking hand" [a training technique, unique to Wing Chun, that enhances one's sensitivity to an opponent's touch, allowing the practitioner to control or manipulate the opponent's arms, thereby rendering the opponent's attempts at attack completely inoperative] in which he attaches his hands to the opponent and subdues him with his eyes shut! At the age of 60 he is still active, and none of his students can even touch him.

Although Bruce Lee was very skillful in Wing Chun, he would have considered himself more a student of the art than an instructor. Indeed, there is no evidence that Yip Man considered Bruce Lee—or anyone other than himself—to be an instructor in Wing Chun. During the time he taught Lee, he had junior students and senior students studying Wing Chun; occasionally the senior students would teach the junior students under the supervision of Yip Man. When Lee finally decided to teach gung fu it, was in America, and he taught his own modified version of Wing Chun. Eventually, however, he discarded virtually all of the Wing Chun methodology, considering the art too restrictive.

8. Since Lee's Chinese language was Cantonese (as opposed to Mandarin or other dialects), the author may have concluded, in error, that he had lived in Canton Province of Mainland China. However, having been born in San Francisco and then spending the first 18 years of his life in the British Crown Colony of Hong Kong, before returning to America to attend university, Lee never lived in China.

Part 2

THE
KATO
YEARS

(1965–1967)

TV Radio Show, October 1966

ROBIN'S NEW LOVE RIVAL

Newest crime fighter on the networks is also a devoted family man, a formidable athlete, and a relentless foe to his enemies.

by "Sara"

There is only one thing wrong with Bruce Lee—he's perfect! He's a perfect husband, a perfect father, and perfectly cast in the role of Kato, the faithful companion of the crime busting Britt Reid in ABC's "Green Hornet." Robin, who has been Batman's side-kick, may find that Kato (Bruce) is a perfectly formidable rival.

Bruce is 145 perfect pounds, and is 5'8". He is 25 years old, born in the United States, but raised in Hong Kong. This is his first starring role, but he inherited his talent for show business from his father, who was a star of Chinese opera and used the name Lee Hoi Chuen. When Bruce was three years old, his family returned to Hong Kong, and he grew up among renowned singers and actors in the performing arts in China.[1]*

Because Bruce is dark, narrow, dashing, he became interested in keeping his body in good form, and he mastered Gung Fu, a respected and ancient art of self-defense which is strictly Oriental. Being Bruce Lee, he is interested in all aspects of anything that interests him, and he decided to learn all about Gung Fu, and has even written books on the sport.[2] It was partly due to his mastery of this difficult skill that Executive Producer William Dozier decided to cast him as Kato. "His ability as a natural athlete provides a good foundation for the role of Kato, who often steps in to save the Green Hornet when they are

---

*Notes for Part 2 begin on page 72.

battling criminals," Dozier explains. But he doesn't deny that Bruce has innate acting ability too. "Bruce has one of the finest natural acting talents that I have seen in my years in the industry," Dozier added.

In 1959, Bruce arrived in Seattle, Washington. He planned to take classes at the University of Washington. He liked this country so much that he decided to stay here. It was a perfectly intelligent decision.

While Bruce was at the university he met Linda Emery, a sensitive, unpretentious, attractive girl. They began a typical college courtship and soon wholesome Linda linked her destiny permanently to exotic Bruce. They now have a 14-month-old son named Brandon.

How can Robin meet such a formidable opponent? Well, fortunately, both boys are really friends, and even live next door to each other. Their wives are friends too. Robin, an expert at Karate, is even thinking of taking up Gung Fu under Bruce's tutelage. But the network

Ready to take on Hollywood: Twenty-five-year-old Bruce Lee in a publicity shot for the then-forthcoming "Green Hornet" TV series.

has forbidden them to exercise with each other—for fear that they may hurt themselves![3]

And how will success affect Bruce Lee? It's not likely to affect him at all. He continues to pursue his sports interests, and plans to participate in tournaments throughout the world.[4] He is also interested in philosophy and spends many hours isolated in research. His personal library supplies him with in-depth studies of Taoism, Zen, Christianity and other religions—as befits a perfectly developed man, with a perfectly developed mind and a perfectly fantastic range of interests and talents. We pity the poor denizens of the underworld who tangle with Kato this season.

Movie Mirror, 1966

MEET BRUCE LEE—THE GREEN HORNET'S BUZZ BOMB

Bruce Lee, a talented young man of only twenty-five, has already accomplished a great many things. You will be seeing quite a lot of him this season in his role of "Kato," the faithful companion to Britt Reid, alias "The Green Hornet." We should like to tell you a few things about Bruce by way of introducing him to you....He was born in the United States and raised in Hong Kong. He is an expert in the art of "Gung Fu," an ancient Chinese method of self-defense, and wears the black belt of Karate, the highest honor awarded to one who has mastered this Japanese method of unarmed self-defense.[5]

Bruce Lee as Kato (right). When "The Green Hornet" TV series premiered on September 16, 1966, North America got its first look at the human dynamo, Bruce Lee (pictured here with series star Van Williams), and the then-unheard-of martial art of gung fu.

His talent for acting was inherited from his father, the famed Lee Hoi Chuen, a star of Chinese opera. It was during an engagement by his father in San Francisco that Bruce was born. His family returned to Hong Kong when he was three but Bruce has always dreamed of revisiting the land of his birth. In 1959 his dream came true. He arrived in

Seattle to enroll in the University of Washington. There, he majored in philosophy and met Miss Linda Emery. The young couple fell in love and were married; they are now the doting parents of a sixteen-month-old son, Brandon.

Bruce could earn a handsome living either teaching philosophy or instructing pupils in "Gung Fu" or Karate. He has written several books on "Gung Fu" and is considered an outstanding authority on the subject. However, his first love has always been the theater. In Hong Kong he grew up among the most famous actors and singers in the performing arts in China.

He believes the role of Kato is just the first of many he hopes will come his way. "There's no business like you know what," he says, "and I am fortunate to love every facet of show business." The Lees make their home in Westwood, a section of Los Angeles. Fittingly enough, their neighbors are the Burt "Robin" Wards!

TV Picture Life, 1966

BRUCE LEE: LOVE KNOWS NO GEOGRAPHY

Bruce and Linda had to overcome many obstacles. But with faith in each other—and the human race—they proved their marriage could last!

by Fredda Dudley Balling

How does it happen that two people from the opposite ends of the earth meet, fall in love, establish a true and contented union, and bring up their children as a triumph of human grace?

Let the story of Bruce Lee (Kato in 20th Century-Fox's

"The Green Hornet") and his wife, Linda Emery Lee, explain it.

Linda was born in Seattle, the younger of two sisters who were brought up in the Baptist faith. The Emerys are what the Hawaiians call "Haole" (Caucasian) or—as it is expressed colloquially, "Garden-variety Americans."[6]

After completing grade and high school in Seattle, Linda matriculated at the University of Washington with the intention of becoming a pediatrician.[7]

Bruce Lee is also an American citizen, having been born in San Francisco. Bruce's beautiful Eurasian mother—one-fourth British, three-fourths Chinese—was touring with Bruce's father when the stork decided to deliver Bruce.[8] The elder Mr. Lee—a famous Chinese opera singer—was appearing in San Francisco's Chinese Opera House at the time.

Bruce was the fourth child of a family to number five children; he has an elder brother and two elder sisters, plus one younger brother. When Bruce was three months old, the family returned to their Hong Kong home.

There Bruce was enrolled in a British private school where, as he says, he learned to pronounce "ox, fox and box" to rhyme with the American pronunciation of "hawks."[9] Not by the remotest stretch of the imagination did Bruce Lee imagine he would ever marry and settle in the United States.

Once he had finished the equivalent of an American high school course, his family sent him to the University of Washington at Seattle, where he chose philosophy as his major.[10] During his sophomore year, he began to pick up a little extra pocket money by teaching the excruciatingly difficult Chinese language, Mandarin dialect, to students who, like himself, were of Chinese ancestry but American birth.[11]

One evening, one of his students brought along a girl friend to audit the language lesson.[12] This girl friend had reddish-brown hair, and—in Bruce's opinion—remarkable eyes. "They were a little blue, a little green, with here and there a fleck of brown. What you call, I think, 'hazel.'" Her name was Linda Emery.

She, in turn, was fascinated by the Mandarin dialect. When given a chance to show what she had learned in one brief session, she demonstrated a singularly sensitive ear and a great vocal ability.

Soon Linda fitted with ease into one of the International groups which enliven every U. S. campus. She was particularly popular with the students from the British Crown Colony of Hong Kong and the Americans of Chinese extraction.[13]

Bruce Lee was also a hit wherever he went. As Linda quickly discovered, Bruce had a natural flair for comedy. When he was asked to explain Chinese Opera, he said, "There are two kinds: Peking opera, which is formal, very stylized, rigidly governed by tradition, and Canton opera, which is more down to earth. As for me, I'd rather watch "The Lone Ranger." That provoked hearty laughter. It was a crack as Stateside as jazz slang.

He also said of Chinese Opera, "All the reactions are Danny Kaye, and all the exits are Jackie Gleason. Class dismissed."

Somehow he was always the center of attention; he amused everyone.

Traveling in the midst of a big college group, Bruce and Linda usually seemed to drift together. One of their group lived at the beach and owned a swimming pool, so water sports were part of the weekend fun. After a splash party, Linda usually combed her long hair back severely and braided it in two pigtails, a practice wonderfully American and slightly funny in Bruce's opinion. Still…he found himself liking it.[14]

After several months of communal dating, Bruce asked Linda one day, "Have you ever been up in the Space Needle?" (A restaurant left over from the Seattle World's Fair.)

"No, I haven't. Have you?"

"Several times. It's great. You can see halfway to Hong Kong. How about dinner there with me tonight?"

Her eyes crinkled at the corners; her smile was instant and delighted. She really wanted to see the view from the Space Needle—with him.[15]

That evening Linda wore her prettiest dress and spent an hour on her hair. Bruce noted the result of Linda's preparation and nodded approval.

Then—solemnly—he handed her a box. "A very small gift," he said.

Nestled in the shredded cellophane was one of those plastic trolls with the hair that never ends. Bruce had divided the wild wig with a center part and had braided two pigtails so firmly that they curled gleefully upward.

Linda shouted with laughter at this lampoon of her own post-swimming hairdo. She knew right then that she would keep the troll forever.

There was, she thought, no one quite like Bruce Lee; he was a fascinating blend of East and West. He had the innate personal dignity characteristic of the Orient; he had a Western sense of humor. He handled American slang as readily as he spoke several Chinese dialects. He was youthfully exuberant, yet there was an air of maturity about him far beyond his years.

Most of all, he was fun to be with; he had marvelously amusing ideas. What other man would take a girl to a Japanese theater to see Samurai movies, explaining them afterward to give insight into a culture far older than that of the Occident, yet often running parallel to Western thought?

Sometimes they drove to the beach and—with rain pelting on the car roof—sat cozily together and talked about the things two young people have discussed since language was invented.[16]

Eventually they approached the theory of marriage. Bruce said that a love affair was one thing, marriage something else. The most satisfactory marriage, he believed, was a friendship caught on fire. In marriage, the excitement of romance was bound to dwindle with the years; in its place must grow the day-to-day companionship that would endure throughout the adventure that is human life. But marriage, unfortunately, is never a contract between two individuals alone. It involves parents, siblings, even a community.

Linda's mother, like every mother, recognized the symptoms of love, saw them in her daughter's bright face, heard them in her daughter's voice and even in her long silences. She said to Linda, "Marriage presents many unexpected problems, even if husband and wife have grown up as next door neighbors, attending the same school and church. Bruce is a fine young man, and I like him. It's just that life with him might present more problems than you can anticipate."

Linda said, "Might the very differences between us solve some problems? Might each of us have more to bring one another because we are, in some ways, half a world apart?"

"Think about it carefully, and discuss it thoroughly with Bruce," was her mother's advice. [17]

Bruce, in his turn, wrote to his father, asking paternal consent to the marriage. Mr. Lee, a true cosmopolite married to a Eurasian, answered that Bruce had his own life to live and his own decisions to make.[18] He was a man now, with a man's responsibility to exercise discretion. The wise father added that his only wish for his son was that he find a good wife, well-suited to his individual needs and tastes.

Bruce Lee:
LOVE KNOWS NO GEOGRAPHY

Bruce and Linda had to overcome many obstacles. But with faith in each other—and the human race—they proved their marriage could last!

The love shared by Bruce and Linda Lee overcame many obstacles, including reporters who often failed to get their facts straight.

Further, he noted the accident of geographical birth had very little to do with a woman's qualification for marriage.

Bruce's mother only wrote one superb sentence: "If she is your choice, she is ours. We welcome her to our family."

And so they were married by the chaplain in the Washington University Chapel at two o'clock on the afternoon of March 17, 1964—St. Patrick's good day, begorra, and rich with luck for all creatures.[19]

Linda wore a sleeveless white dress, street length, with a jewel neckline and a pleated skirt. Bruce wore the conventional business suit, and slid a plain platinum wedding band on his bride's finger.[20]

Linda's mother and her grandmother were her witnesses, and Bruce's best man was his buddy, Taky (pronounced Tocky) Kimura.[21]

Because their decision to marry had been made swiftly, there had been no time to choose a wedding bouquet, or to order a cake, or to observe any of the rituals of either Orient or Occident. It didn't matter to two of the happiest people on earth.

They rented an apartment and Linda was attending courses in Chinese cookery when there occurred a simple incident that was to change their lives forever.[22] In Long Beach, California, a Gung Fu tournament was scheduled, and Bruce—an expert—was asked to give a demonstration of some of the principles of the art, a highly advanced form of Karate.[23]

Now, pay close attention to the following developments, because they are a little complicated: Jay Sebring, probably Hollywood's best-known hair-stylist for men, is a Gung Fu fan. One of Mr. Sebring's clients is famed producer William Dozier. In the course of one of their conversations, Jay Sebring regaled the producer with a report of the tournament, particularly the stunning ability of one Bruce Lee.

Bill Dozier was casting a projected TV series, sort of a Charley Chan scare-'em, so he needed a wiry combatant to serve as Number One Son. He asked to see the movies taken of Bruce's performance by the director of the tournament.

Bruce was sent a round-trip ticket to confer with Mr. Dozier in Hollywood. He made the flight in a slightly dazed condition and was still dazed on the return trip because he had been placed under five-year contract by Bill Dozier.[24]

In short, the original TV series never materialized, but "The Green Hornet" did.

Bruce and Linda moved to Hollywood, where their son was born in February, 1965. He was given two names: Brandon, because

Bruce just happened to like the name, and Gok Ho, which in Chinese means "National Hero."[25]

Brandon Gok Ho had a mop of black hair when he was born, but as most newborn babies do, he shed it quickly and is now a golden blond with magnificent licorice button eyes. He is a handsome meeting of two cultures: possibly the only blond Chinese baby in the world, and probably one of the few brown-eyed youngsters of Swedish-English extraction. He has a button nose and a dimple in his chin and he wins the heart, instantly, of everyone who comes into the Lee home.

Grandfather Lee learned of the new grandson, then died suddenly two days later.[26] Bruce, having welcomed his son, flew home to bid his father a final farewell. His one comfort during those grievous days was the thought of his father's knowledge of the new member of the family.

But there was someone who needed comfort even more than Bruce did: his mother. And so, when Brandon was three months old, he and his parents made the same trip that Bruce had made at that age. The Lees flew to Hong Kong to present their son to his grandmother.

No Oriental woman ever sheds tears in public, because the sight of her sorrow might bring unhappiness to others; by custom she may succumb to emotion only when she is alone.

However, when Brandon's grandmother took him into her arms, she permitted tears to slide across her cheeks because they were good tears, happy tears, which could inspire only similar tears in a beholder.

Brandon had proved to be a many-splendored blessing. For Linda, Hong Kong was Ali Baba's treasure house. In spite of the blazing heat of Hong Kong's early summer, she bought a dozen dresses; she ordered suits and coats made to order.[27] "I feel like a princess preparing for a trip around the world," she confided to Bruce.

And one evening she felt like an Empress when Bruce handed her a pair of velvet boxes. One held a white gold wedding ring set with five generous diamonds and the other revealed a brilliant solitaire.[28]

"The rings we didn't have time to order when we decided to get married," explained Bruce.

They drove to the world-famed Repulse Bay Hotel for luncheon, and they drove to the Carleton Hotel on the Kowloon side to watch sunset dye the waters of Hong Kong harbor magenta and crimson and purple. They rode the tram to Victoria Peak, and they went fishing in a quiet bay.

Another surprise was the firecrackers. The first time Linda heard what she thought was gunfire, she burst into tears.[29] The Red hordes must have landed. Then it turned out that a new restaurant was opening, and evil spirits were being driven away. After that she delighted in the pop, snap, crackle, zap and zowie whenever someone celebrated or won at the races.

Now and then, as she walked along the streets faintly scented with joss, she heard a word that she recognized. She was, she realized, fitting into a new life—one remarkably comfortable and filled with contentment.

When the Lees returned to Hollywood, one of Linda's friends observed, "Do you realize that you have an accent? You sound exactly like Bruce."

"Why not?" asked Mrs. Lee. "We're a family."

All of which tells something wonderful about the world in which we live.

TV and Movie Screen, 1966

BRUCE LEE: "OUR MIXED MARRIAGE BROUGHT US A MIRACLE OF LOVE"

by Fredda Dudley Balling

Bruce Lee and his wife, Linda, are the parents of one of destiny's children. His name is Brandon; he is Oriental and Occidental; he has eyes like ripe black cherries; his hair is blond; his personality is a fascinating blend of the thoughtfulness of the East and vigor of the West. Bruce says of his sturdy son, "I don't know where he's going—but he's on his way."

Bruce himself, is an American citizen, born in San Francisco of a celebrated Chinese father and a beautiful Eurasian mother; Linda was born in Seattle, the daughter of Swedish-English parents. These diverse blood lines have met in Brandon Lee, and the result is superb.

Yet, there are people who—once they know Bruce well enough —are emboldened to ask, "How will you bring up your son in a world in which prejudice is everywhere?"

Bruce shakes his head, smiling. "No problem. Brandon is being brought up in the midst of two cultures. There are good points in Chinese culture; there are good points in Occidental culture. He will be taught to take some principles from one, some from the other.

"Brandon will learn that Oriental culture and Occidental culture are not mutually exclusive, but mutually dependent. Neither would be remarkable if it were not for the existence of the other.

"Much of what Brandon will learn from Occidental culture he will acquire, first from his mother, then from schooling. Much of what Brandon will learn from Oriental culture will come from me, and I will have learned it from Gung Fu, in which the Zen influence is strong.[30] Zen has derived many of its concepts from the Chinese belief in balance: Yin, which is feminine and gentle, and Yang, which is masculine and firm. Having accepted that basic idea, another must be added: there is no such thing as pure Yin or pure Yang. Gentleness should cloak firmness; firmness should be modified by gentleness. No woman should follow passively. She must learn that there is an active way of following. She must have what the Occidentals call 'backbone.' By the same reasoning, no man should be totally firm; his resolve must be softened by compassion.

"Once Brandon has learned to understand Yin and Yang, he will know that nothing can be secured by extremes. For instance, the haircuts worn by many boys at this time are not haircuts at all, but disguises. The fashion cannot last, because it is extreme and will soon tire the wearer and the beholder. Possibly the beholder more quickly, but a vast boredom for all in any case.

"Only sober moderation lasts, and that persists through all time. Only the mid-part of anything is preserved because the pendulum must have balance, and the mid-part *is* the balance.

"There is another bit of Chinese philosophy that has a bearing on problems common to all humankind. We say, 'The oak tree is mighty, yet it will be destroyed by a mighty wind because it resists the elements; the bamboo bends with the wind, and by bending, survives.'

"We advance the idea by saying, 'Be pliable. When a man is living, he is soft and pliable; when he is dead, he becomes rigid. Pliability is life; rigidity is death, whether one speaks of man's body, his mind or his spirit.'

"We also say, 'Be like water; it is the softest element on earth, yet it penetrates the hardest rock. It has no shape of its own, yet it can take any shape in which it is placed. In a cup, it becomes the shape of the cup. In a vase, it takes the shape of the vase and curls about the stems of flowers. Water may seem to move in contradiction, even uphill, but it chooses any way open to it so that it may reach the sea. It may flow swiftly or it may flow slowly, but its purpose is inexorable, its destiny sure.'"

What will Bruce teach his son about money, the preoccupation of so many Americans? Bruce says, "Money of itself has no explicit nature. Money is what one makes of it. A child must be taught early that money is only a means, a type of usefulness, an implement. Like all instruments, it has certain purposes, but it will not do everything. One must learn how to use it, what it will do, but above all what it will not do.

"I profited from my father's philosophy about money. He used to tell me, 'If you make 10 dollars this year, always think to yourself that next year you may make only five dollars—so be prepared.'"

Next, what will Bruce tell his son about love and marriage, in the face of statistics applying to Occidental divorce?

"Easy. I will tell him, and Linda and I will demonstrate for him, that marriage is a friendship, a partnership based solidly upon ordinary, everyday occurrences. Marriage is breakfast in the morning, work during the day—the husband at his work, the wife at hers—dinner at night and quiet evenings together talking, reading or watching television. Marriage is caring for children, watching over them in sickness, training them in the way they must go, sharing worry about them and pride in them.

"Courtship is not always the proper prelude to marriage. During courtship, two people who are attracted to each other seek exciting things to do. They go dancing, they dine at fine resturants, go to museums. They get to know all the diversions in their particular geographic locality, but they do not get to know one another.

Brandon is being brought up in the midst of two cultures....He will be taught to take some principles from one, some from the other. Brandon will learn that Oriental culture and Occidental culture are not mutually exclusive, but mutually dependent. Neither would be remarkable if it were not for the existence of the other.

"I think it is true that many successful American marriages are made in college. There, each has a task and each can evaluate the will and the zeal with which the other approaches responsibility. In a college situation which demands application of intention, but flexibility of approach, one can learn much about one's fellow student's success with learning techniques. Brandon will attend an American university, of course, but he will also be trained in Hong Kong.[31]

"You see, nothing is superior in every respect; the Occidental education is excellent in some ways, the Oriental in others. You will say, 'This finger is better for one purpose; this finger is better for another.' But the entire hand is better for all purposes."

There is always a great deal of Occidental conversation about "happiness" and "finding one's self." Can a recipe for happiness and finding oneself be provided for a child?

Bruce, Linda, and Brandon united in a moment of peace.

Bruce says, "There is too much Occidental tendency to look inward at one's own moods, and to try to evaluate them. To stand on the outside and try to look inside is futile; whatever was there will go away. This also applies to a nebulous thing described as 'happiness.' To try to identify it is like turning on a light to look at darkness. Analyze it, and it is gone. We have a Zen parable that tells of a man who said, 'Master, I must seek liberation.'

"The teacher asked, 'And who binds you?'

"The student answered, 'I do not know. Perhaps I bind myself.'

"So the teacher said, 'In that case, why seek liberation of me? In summer we sweat; in winter we shiver.'

"So the student thought, 'He is speaking of a secret place where our only problem is the seasons of the year.'

"I will teach Brandon that each man binds himself; the fetters are ignorance, laziness, preoccupation with self, and fear. He must liberate himself, while accepting the fact that we are of this world, so that 'In summer we sweat; in winter we shiver.'"

When Brandon meets up with intolerance and hostility, how will he react because of the preparation Bruce has given him?

Bruce shrugs and says, "There is a Chinese folk story that applies. There was a fine butcher who used the same knife year after year, yet it never lost its delicate, precise edge. After a life-time of service, it was still as useful and effective as when it was new. When asked how he had preserved his knife's fine edge, he said, 'I follow the line of the hard bone. I do not attempt to cut it, nor to smash it, nor to contend with it in any way. That would only destroy my knife.'

"In daily living, one must follow the course of the barrier. To try to assail it will only destroy the instrument. And no matter what some people will say, barriers are not the experience of any one person, or any one group of persons. They are the universal experience.

"I will also teach Brandon that everyone—no matter who he is or where—must know from childhood that whatever occurs, does not happen if the occurrence isn't allowed to come into the mind.

"In Chinese variety stores we have a weighted dog, like your weighted clowns, which points out a moral: 'Fall down nine times, but rise again ten times.' To refuse to be cast down, that is the lesson.

"More than instructing Brandon in such precepts, I will teach him to walk on.[32] Walk on and he will see a new view. Walk on and he will see the birds fly. Walk on and leave behind all things that would dam up the inlet, or clog the outlet, of experience.

"I'll tell him, not that he must enter into anything with a totality of spirit. Something must be held back. The Occidental homily is 'Don't put all your eggs in one basket,' but it is spoken of material things. I refer to the emotional, intellectual, spiritual.

"I can illustrate my beliefs by what I practice in my own life. I have a lot to learn as an actor. I am learning. I am investing much of myself in it, but not all. Gung Fu is also a vital part of my life.

"Finally, through all Brandon's education will run the Confucianist philosophy that the highest standards of conduct consist of treating others as you wish to be treated, plus loyalty, intelligence and the fullest development of the individual in the five chief relationships of life: government and those who are governed, father and son, elder and younger brother, husband and wife, friend and friend. Equipped in that way, I don't think Brandon can go far wrong."

The feeling in Hollywood is that, far from going wrong, Brandon will be so admirable a citizen that Bruce and Linda should give this country about a dozen youngsters like him, heirs to the best of two cultures.

Chinese Bruce Lee says of his American child:

"I WANT MY SON TO BE A MIXED-UP KID!"

by Flora Rand

On ABC-TV's "The Green Hornet," Bruce Lee may sometimes don a mask of the utmost Oriental inscrutability, as he co-stars in the role of Kato. In real life, his engaging smile beams from ear to ear as he tells you of his happily "mixed-up" marriage to the beautiful Linda and brags of their handsome son. "Our first child is a blond, grey-eyed Chinaman," Bruce twinkles proudly, "maybe the only one around."

As he speaks of little Brandon, his chest swells fit to burst his tailored suit. "I'd like to send him back to Hong Kong to school when he's about five, to stay until he's about 11—but I'm not sure Linda would stand for that!" The pride in his voice deepens as he mentions his wife, and he spreads his hands in a gesture of surrender.

"I guess Linda might not let Brandon go so far away without her. But, as the next best thing, maybe we can bring a Chinese woman here to live with us and take care of him. He's learning to speak Chinese now—he can already say Daddy!—but it's hard to become proficient in a language if you only get to use it occasionally."

Bruce Lee's philosophy (like his well-tailored suit, his cuff links and his sapphire ring) is an exquisite import from Hong Kong. His slang-tinged vernacular is as jazzy and Western as a Sousa march. He has a snappy, up-to-the-minute, Hollywood-approved style, but immediately beneath the veneer, he's thoroughly, totally, completely Chinese. And he's thoroughly, totally and completely proud of the fact.

American by birth (and by accident), Bruce is Chinese by breeding and upbringing. He was born in the United States only because his father, a noted Chinese opera singer, was in this country on tour at the moment. Bruce was returned to Hong Kong when he was three months old and lived there until he entered college at the University of Washington in Seattle, in the land of his birth.

His wife, by contrast, is the former Linda Emery, a Seattle blonde who was swept off her feet by her lively Oriental suitor during two years of campus courtship. As a consequence, their son— now just 19 months old—is in a peculiarly fortunate position.

Instead of being heir to one great culture, he's heir to two, and his parents—especially his father—aren't going to let him forget it for a minute. Bruce Lee actually, literally *wants* his son to be a "mixed-up kid"—because then he'll have the very best of two worlds, both East and West. Brandon may learn Gung Fu (the ancient Oriental art of self-defense at which Bruce is such an expert) before he learns good old American baseball, but he'll learn them both equally well.

The same goes for the Baptist faith versus Buddhism. Brandon will get a chance to sample each—along with any other religions which interest him—in the hope that he'll draw the best from every philosophy before he firmly accepts one as his own.[33]

Bruce himself grew up in a wealthy household and—despite some privations during the war years—remembers his Hong Kong boyhood as a period of happy comfort, if not downright luxury. Though his father was Buddhist and his mother Catholic, this never presented any conflict.

"When my mother went to church on Sunday," says Bruce, "my father sat at home. This didn't seem to worry her—and it didn't worry my father that she was sending me to a Catholic school."

In this school, Bruce mastered some English, but he didn't become confirmed in the Catholic faith. Instead, he developed a keen, wide-ranging interest in all religions and philosophies, from Taoism to Protestantism.

Surrounded at home by the traditions of his ancestors, he acquired a deep respect for the heritage which had produced him. Even so, he was intrigued by thoughts of the United States, the actual country of his birth. So, when he was ready for college, that's where he headed.

And that's where he met Linda, a lovely, dignified girl who, according to Bruce, "is more Oriental than some of the Chinese I know. She had a great many Oriental friends in high school," he explains, "and she had acquired some of their attitudes, I guess. Anyway, she's quiet. Calm. She doesn't yak-yak-yak all the time like some women. She's really a wonderful person."

They were never really engaged, during their two-year courtship at the University of Washington. "We just suddenly decided, *This is it*, he grins. "So why have an engagement? When we decided to get married, we married. Just like that. I remember going over to Linda's house to tell her parents that we wanted to marry. They weren't too happy at first, because they thought I was going to carry her away, across the Pacific. And, to tell you the truth that was what we'd planned to do—go back to Hong Kong.

Linda and I aren't one *and* one. We are *two* halves *that make a* whole. *You have to apply yourself to be a family—two halves fitted together are more efficient than either half would ever be alone!*

"Linda's mother and father were a little worried, especially because of the situation in Vietnam and Red China. But they were pretty nice about the whole thing."

Worried or not, the bride's parents arranged for the ceremony in the church of their faith. Bruce thinks it was Baptist, but he's not sure. "I wasn't thinking too much about what kind of preacher we had. I was only interested in getting married!"

Although the pull of Hong Kong was strong, the young bridegroom delayed a return to his homeland because of another compulsion. "I felt that I had to accomplish something personally,"

Bruce says now. "What would I have done if I'd gone to Hong Kong? Nothing. I wouldn't have had to do a thing for myself.

"I could have said, 'Bring tea,' and the servant would have brought tea. Just like that. I could have spent every day in leisure. And, in one way, I would have liked it. I would have enjoyed the ease and luxury. I don't have any great *longing* to work.

"On the other hand, I wanted to do something for myself—to bring honor to my own name. In Hong Kong, if I rode in a big car, people only said, 'There's Bruce Lee in his old man's car.' Whatever I did, it was a reflection of what my family had already accomplished.

"When I went home, I wanted to be able to show my mother a handful of money and say, 'Here, take $10,000—or $50,000! I *earned* it. Help yourself. It's a present from me."

Between Two Worlds

The fact that Bruce still has a longing for Hong Kong is evident in his desire to send Brandon there for some of his formative years. But his own plans to return have been altered, at least temporarily, by his plunge into acting.

Bruce is expert at several sports. While Gung Fu is his primary hobby (he's already teaching it to Brandon), he's also so good at karate that he participated in an international karate tournament in Long Beach, California, in 1964—and it was there that he was discovered by a Hollywood talent scout.[34]

Bruce had more than his athletic progress to recommend him. Bill Dozier, producer of "The Green Hornet," says of him, "He has one of the finest natural acting talents I've seen in my years in the industry."

So now Bruce has a brand-new career to contend with, as well as a mixed-up marriage and a (hopefully) mixed-up kid! "Basically, human traits are the same everywhere," he says wisely. But he also recognizes that, because he and Linda spring from sharply divergent backgrounds, they must work to produce in Brandon, a happy blending of the two.

"Naturally, I like the Chinese culture better but the American is more practical. Brandon will have *both*," he notes happily.

As for his relationship with Linda, Bruce thinks they have each made some concessions in keeping with the other's point of view. For example, he's come a long way in his mastery of English— while she's been learning Chinese with the help of a tape recorder.

"When I got to this country," Bruce confesses, "I still didn't know English very well. But no—language was never a problem between Linda and me! We could always make each other understand."

As far as eating is concerned, they've no problems, either, because Linda is crazy about Chinese food. In fact, she attended classes to learn how to prepare it properly.

"Oh, sure," Bruce laughs, "we compromise sometimes and eat American food. Like, for instance, would you believe steak and fried rice?"

Although Bruce is happy to make concessions in some areas, he hopes his son will grow up with totally Chinese respect for his parents. "It may not be as easy to develop that attitude here," he admits, "as it would be in Hong Kong. That's one reason I'd like for Brandon to go to school there for a while, so he could better learn to respect his family and its traditions—and that way gain more self-respect.

"There, because of the strong family relationship, we don't have the delinquency, the smart-alecks, that we have here. Hong Kong is a British colony, you know, and is about half Western. Even so, a Chinese boy growing up there knows that if he disgraces himself, he brings disgrace upon all his kin—upon a great circle of people. And I think this is good.

"There was a time when a Chinese son could never— never—contradict his father, but that's no longer true except in the very rigid, old families. Things are a little more relaxed than that in most households. But Chinese children still don't argue with their parents.

"No, my father never struck me—though my mother sometimes spanked me good!—and I'm not planning to strike Brandon. I think a father can control the situation by swinging with it. You know what I mean?

"I will play with my son and joke with my son, but business is business. When the subject is a serious one, you don't go around trying to keep from hurting his feelings. You say what must be said and set the rules which must be set without worrying about whether he likes it or not. I know, though, that in the long run he'll like it."

Bruce definitely feels that the approach to child psychology which works so successfully in Hong Kong will work just as well in Los Angeles. And how does Linda react to Bruce's views?

"Oh, she's a good Chinese wife," he grins. "And in a Chinese household, the husband is the boss. Linda and I aren't *one* and *one*," he emphasizes seriously. "We are two *halves* that make a *whole*. You have to apply yourself to be a family—two halves fitted together are more efficient than either half would ever be alone!"

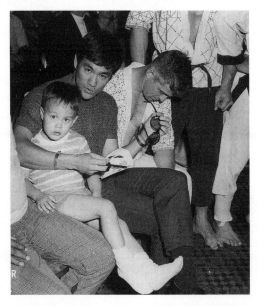

Bruce Lee and his son Brandon were virtually inseparable. The elder Lee took his son to all sorts of outings, including martial arts tournaments.

Washington Daily News, 1966

"GREEN HORNET" STAR DISCUSSES NEW SERIES

by Harry Kershner and Hans Gordon

Bruce Lee, the personable, athletic young man who plays Kato in ABC's new "The Green Hornet" series was in town yesterday and said he hoped the show would do as well in the ratings as the same network's "Batman" series. (Van Williams will star as "The Green Hornet." He and Kato will battle against crime on WMAL-TV, Ch. 7, Fridays, from 7:30-8:00 PM.)

In answer to the charge of imitation leveled against his series, the handsome San Francisco native answered, "Our show is completely different from 'Batman.' 'The Green Hornet' is a James Bondish type straight action show. There won't be any kind of 'camp' humor."

The format has been modernized from its radio days. It will abound with gimmicks: a flashy black car with attached rockets (the "Black Beauty"), a secret elevator hidden in the fireplace of the "The Green Hornet's" home, a gas gun, and the fantastic "Hornet Sting," a weapon almost as valuable as the ever-faithful Kato.

Mr. Lee was discovered by William Dozier (also the producer of "Batman") at an international karate tournament last year.

His specialty is Gung Fu, an Oriental off-shoot of karate and judo, which he describes as a "fluid and purely offensive" fighting technique in comparison to the "ritualistic, defensive" maneuvers of karate.[35] It will be demonstrated often in the series.

"The Green Hornet" will debut Sept. 9, when Al Hirt's version of "Flight of the Bumble Bee" (what else?) will be heard as the theme music for the dynamic duo of the insect world. Whatever the artistic success of their series, Lee, Dozier and friends should be seeing a lot of "green" for some time to come.

Seattle newspaper, 1966

ACTOR IS GUNG-HO FOR GUNG-FU

by C. J. Skreen

It may not produce any Nobel Prizes for the University of Washington, but the local school can at least claim credit for contributing to the world one of the most famous manservants since Crusoe's Man Friday.

The contribution in question is Bruce Lee, who plays Kato, the faithful aide of Britt Reid in ABC's television version of the old radio serial, "The Green Hornet."

Lee, who was a philosophy major at the university from 1960 to 1963, is in town for the holidays with his wife and 22-month-old son, Brandon, visiting her family. She is the former Linda Emery, ex-Garfield High School yell queen.

To those who may not regard "The Green Hornet" as the greatest thing to happen to broadcasting since Liberace donned se-quins, it should be noted that the TV series is based on the exploits of a crusading newspaper editor–publisher who dons green clothes and turns crime-fighter at night. For nine years in the 1930's, the Hornet was bigger in publishing circles than the *Chicago Tribune*'s Colonel McCormick.

The revival of the radio show in TV form is a direct offspring of Batman's success, being a product of the same producer, William Dozier. As such it has had its problems this season, facing the com-petition of the new "Tarzan" series and "The Wild, Wild West" on Friday evenings.

The Hornet moved off to a slow start but seems to be holding its own at this point. It is No.1 in its time slot in the Seattle market and is set to ride out the season.

Discussing the show's problems, Lee said that the series had been played "too straight" and that "a lighter, James Bond touch" would be the new approach.

"If we are renewed next season," Lee added, "the producers hope to expand it to an hour. The show has simply been crammed with too many characters."

Lee's role as the crime-fighting Kato requires considerable physical agility but the personable, short-statured young actor (26) is more than up to the demands.

Having lived in Hong Kong for the first 18 years of his life before coming to Seattle, Lee is a life-long devotee of Gung-Fu, an Oriental method of self-defense that is an advanced form of karate and ju-jitsu.

The Chinese master of mayhem owes both his marriage and his first television exposure to Gung Fu. While he was instructing a course in the manly (and womanly) art of self-defense on University Way, one of his students turned out to be his future wife. "The Green Hornet" star also starred in a Gung Fu series of lectures on Channel 9 (will the wonders of educational TV ever cease?).

Lee is so gung-ho on Gung-Fu, in fact, that he is opening a school in Los Angeles shortly to teach the sport and already has an instructor, Taky Kimura, working in Seattle.[36]

Lee offers a modified version of Gung-Fu on "The Green Hornet" but he admits the accent is on flash and fanciness ("We have to slow down in the fight scenes").

Lee is scheduled to appear on "The Buddy Webber Show" Thursday morning over Channel 4 and it is possible we may get an unexpurgated edition of his Oriental pastime. Webber, you may recall, runs a segment of the Jack La Lanne physical fitness show on his program.

With both Lee and La Lanne aboard, this may be the last of "The Buddy Webber Show."

Unknown newspaper, 1966

HOLY HERO, BATMAN! DON'T LET THE GUNG-FU GET YOU

by Richard K. Shull

HOLLYWOOD—Van Williams, dressed in an iridescent green topcoat and matching hat, with a Kelly Green mask over half his face, explained, "We're not camp." Perhaps it's normal to run around in such an outfit and drive a car that buzzes?

"Well, you can't say we're straight, but then you can say James Bond is camp," he said. "With The Green Hornet, there has to be gimmicks for the kids. The merchandising is where the money is."

So it is that one of America's older crime fighters is coming to TV next month. At Desilu-Culver Studio, Williams and the rest of "The Green Hornet" troupe were working wearily behind schedule to churn out episodes of the new series.

The temperature was in the high 90s inside the stage, but the role called for Williams to wear his heavy green outfit, symbol of the secret crime fighter.

Between takes of a scene in which Williams was appearing with a group of men, he confided what most everyone already knew—"The Green Hornet" is a contemporization of "The Lone Ranger." That's what it is. "We don't play it for laughs, it's straight and serious. There's some humor and some parallel to Batman. You can compare all you want to. That's good. So tune in and compare," he said as he went back to work.

Outside the stage, his TV partner, Bruce Lee, who plays "the faithful Oriental servant, Kato," was standing barechested attempting to escape the heat. Lee, 25, will bring a new system of fighting to the masses this fall—Gung-Fu.

Like Karate Only Different

"Unlike karate, Gung-Fu is an Oriental offensive system using both the hands and feet. And with shoes on, in the show, I'll be the Green Hornet's weapon," Lee said.

And he was quick to point out, Kato will have an elevated status in the TV series, "The Green Hornet and Kato are a partnership. It's not a 'Yes, Mr. Blimp,' relationship. I'm Chinese, but the name, Kato, is Japanese. But Westerners won't know the difference," Lee said. "The producer is lucky to find a Chinaman who can say, Britt Reid (the Green Hornet's public name)," Lee laughed.

Lee was born in San Francisco while his father, a star of Chinese

Opera, was performing there. His parents returned to Hong Kong when Bruce was three months old. He lived in China and Hong Kong until 1959, when he came to this country to study at the University of Washington. He returned to Hong Kong for about 6 months in 1963 and again for most of last year.[37]

"My real line is teaching Gung-Fu. I have schools in Seattle, Oakland and Hong Kong.[38] I have karate instructors studying under me," he said.

In 1964, Lee demonstrated his art at a world karate tournament in Los Angeles. Jay Sebring, the men's hair stylist, saw the performance and touted Lee to TV producer Bill Dozier. Dozier kept him in mind and when he started work on "The Green Hornet," he picked Lee as the logical Kato.

So what is Gung-Fu?

He Handles It with His Feet

"It's not like karate, where they grunt and yip, and where they miss and chop the table in two with their hand. Gung-Fu is simplicity. You approach your victim (he said, approaching) and ba-boom-boom-boom"—almost too fast to see, each foot struck out twice dusting off my chin, Adam's apple and chest.

"I had to slow down my movements for the show," he laughed. "They were too quick for the camera."

Gung-Fu also employs the hands and arms. He exhibited his forearms which had knots of muscle larger than the receiving end of a Louisville slugger, and twice as hard.

"I work out three times a week," Lee said. "I do two finger push ups with one hand."

About that time, a car rolled by with Adam (Batman) West in the passenger seat. Lee yelled and waved to him. West stared blankly and waved back.

"Adam couldn't see without his glasses," Lee explained. "Now Van Williams and I, we both wear contact lenses."

So it is among TV super crime-fighters.

The Tribune, 1966

TV MAILBOX

Q—I would like to know something about Bruce Lee (Kato on "The Green Hornet"). How tall is he? Can he really fight Karate? A—Lee is 5 feet 7 or thereabouts. He does not fight Karate at all. He is a Gung Fu expert. Gung Fu is a Chinese art of self-defense which has some similarities to Karate, but it stresses relaxation and a sort of philosophical mental attitude. That seems generally sensible to me; since I generally lose fights, it would help to be philosophical about it. Lee used to teach Gung Fu in Oakland, and wrote a book on the subject. His former partner, J. Y. Lee, sent me a copy of it, but I haven't much use for it, as I hate violence. I'll send the book to the first person who writes for it. I'll also send a copy of my pamphlet, "How to Avoid Fights Without Actually Chickening Out."

The Washington Post, August 30, 1966

BATMAN'S BOY HAS BLACK BELT RIVAL

by Leroy F. Aarons

The newest challenge to Robin, the Boy Wonder, is Bruce Lee, a young actor and karate expert who will portray Kato, faithful sidekick of the Green Hornet, when that latest entry in the Batman sweepstakes buzzes onto ABC Television Sept. 9.

For those trivia dropouts who never heard of "The Green Hornet," it was an immensely popular radio serial during the 1940's, featuring a newspaper publisher by day turned masked crime fighter by night. In those days, Kato was a subservient Oriental chauffeur whose big moments came when Britt Reid, the publisher, barked, "My car, Kato," and Kato answered, "Yessuh, Mistah Blitt."

Not so in the streamlined ABC version, says Lee, a muscular, self-contained young Chinese who was in town the other day on a whirlwind promotion tour.

"I'm going to be more of a companion and partner of the Green Hornet," he said in slightly accented English. "Actually, with my background in Gung-Fu (a classical form of karate), they are making me the weapon. I'll be doing all the fighting. Once in a while the Green Hornet will throw some punches, but when he goes into it, it's the old American swing. I'll do all the chopping and kicking, and when it's necessary to get a gun out of a guy's hand from a distance, I'll be throwing darts."

Lee, educated and articulate, was actually a little leery when William Dozier, the producer who brought Batman to the airwaves, approached him about the Kato role.

"It sounded at first like typical houseboy stuff," he said. "I tell Dozier, 'Look if you sign me up with all that pigtail and hopping around jazz, forget it.' In the past, the typical casting has been that kind of stereotype. Like with the Indians. You never see a human being Indian on television."

Lee, 25, came to the Kato role via a circuitous route that involved a karate tournament and a Hollywood barber. Born in San Francisco, he was raised in Hong Kong, where his father was a star of the Chinese opera.

Lee was a child actor in Chinese films but his prime interest was Gung-Fu, in which he became an expert, a teacher and author of several books. In 1964, he competed in the International Karate Tournament in Long Beach, Calif., and was seen by Jay Sebring, a barber who specializes in male coiffures at $10 a cut.[39]

Sebring was cutting Dozier's hair one day when Dozier mentioned that he was looking for someone to play the lead in a television adventure series about the son of Charlie Chan. Sebring told him about Lee, and Dozier, after seeing films of the karate matches, became interested.[40]

The Charlie Chan series never materialized, but when "The Green Hornet" package got to the planning stages, Dozier immediately thought of Lee. Lee, an ambitious fellow, is now hoping that his Cinderella story will lead to a solid gold slipper.

It sounded at first like typical houseboy stuff. I told Dozier, "Look, if you sign me up with all that pigtail and hopping around jazz, forget it." In the past, the typical casting has been that kind of stereotype. Like with the Indians. You never see a human being Indian on television.

Washington Star, 1966

A SWINGING "KATO" PAYS A VISIT

by Bernie Harrison

I've had my doubts about Robin the "Boy Wonder," on "Batman," who has always appeared to me to look suspiciously like a couple of carrier boys we once had who couldn't carry the Sunday edition from the sidewalk to the door without making an Alpine expedition of it.

I've no doubts about the lithe young actor, Bruce Lee, who'll be playing "Kato" to "The Green Hornet," the new ABC-TV series that premieres Friday, Sept. 9. Over lunch yesterday at Duke Zeibert's with Bruce and one of his Washington friends, Jhoon Rhee, of the Tae Kwon Do Institute, we fell to discussing the critique of actor Robert Phillips (last Thursday's Star), an ex-Marine and self-defense instructor who felt that karate was much overrated. "Karate," Phillips said, "is a hoax. None of these alleged killer techniques are any deadlier than the basic caveman movements of the common streetfighter."

"There is much truth to what he says," Lee said, "much that is incorrect." The 25-year-old actor who once taught Gung-Fu, a subject allied to karate, at the University of Washington, said that "the distinction that must be made is between the classical instruction, and the practical. That's all he was really saying."

"Here," he said, "feel my forearm."

I felt. Like steel.

On "The Green Hornet," he said, "I'm the fellow who takes care of the villains. And it's done quickly." He demonstrated with a couple of fast chops and swings, scattering my French fries and aplomb.

Lee is naturally directing the fight sequences, until the directors become alert to the possibilities. "The Hornet," he insisted, "won't be another 'Batman.' It'll be straight—which sounds funny when you consider the Hornet's car, the scanning machine, and other devices. But we'll be more like James Bond than Batman." The theme (honest) will be "Flight of the Bumblebee."

To old-time listeners to the "Hornet" on radio, you should know that Kato, who started out as the hero's faithful Japanese manservant and became, the week after Pearl Harbor, his faithful Filipino manservant, is now only vaguely identified as Oriental. Lee, who plays the part, was born in San Francisco while his father, Lee Hoi-Chuen, a star of the Chinese opera, was appearing there. Lee grew up in Hong Kong but after one visit to his birthplace in 1959, decided to remain in this country. He met his wife, Linda Emery, at the University of Washington and they have a 15-month-old son, Brandon. He participated in the International Karate Tourney at Long Beach, Calif., two years ago, and was persuaded to take up acting.

Wistfully, he says he'd like to see the Hornet and Kato develop a relationship not unlike that of Culp and Cosby.[41]

By the way, Lee can pronounce his "r's—when I put my mind to it."

GREEN HORNET'S HELPER USED TO BUZZ AROUND "U"

by Ed Quimby

Two of the most successful crime-fighters in the business were edu-cated at the University of Washington. One is Batman, who last year began fighting crime for television. The other is Kato, fighting crime this year for his first time.

Kato is the Green Hornet's faithful companion and able-bod-ied assistant. He was known in the Registrar's Office as Bruce Lee.

Kato, alias Bruce Lee, entered the university in 1961. He began as a drama major, but later became a pre-major in Arts and Sciences.[42]

He took a number of drama courses, and after changing ma-jors took several courses in Chinese philosophy. He left the univer-sity in the spring of 1964 to fight crime for television.[43]

Kato, who often steps in to save the Green Hornet when they are battling nefarious criminals, is an expert at Gung-Fu, an Orien-tal method of self-defense. He has participated in Gung-Fu tourna-ments throughout the world, and has written several books on the subject.

As if Gung-Fu weren't devastating enough, Kato knows Karate. He participated in the 1964 International Karate Tourna-ment at Long Beach, Calif.

A man of diverse talents, he was Hong Kong's 1961 Cha Cha Champion.[44] A girl who was in his dancing class here at the univer-sity said "He was cute, talented, and he had a good personality," but added "He was a fast talker." They sometimes stayed after class and danced. "He wanted to teach me to Cha Cha," she said.

The executive producer of "The Green Hornet," William

Dozier, said "Bruce has one of the finest natural acting talents that I have seen. He is a handsome young man who fits the character perfectly."

Bruce Lee was born in San Francisco. His father, Lee Hoi-Chuen, a famous star of Chinese opera, was appearing in the Bay City at the time. His parents returned to Hong Kong when their son was 3 months old, and Bruce Lee grew up among singers and actors of the performing arts in China.

He returned to the United States to attend the University of Washington. He met his wife, Linda Emery, at the university. They have a son, Brandon.

Although wrapped up in Gung-Fu and acting, Kato is still interested in philosophy. He has volumes on Zen Buddhism, Taoism, Christianity and other religions.

If Gung-Fu doesn't work, he can always pray.

The St. Paul Dispatch, July 18, 1968

DEADLY SIMPLE FIGHTER

by P. M. Clepper

I can tell the producers of "The Green Hornet" how to improve their show—even before it's on the air. What they should do is let the Hornet's sidekick, Kato, write his own dialogue. If they did that, I predict they'd have another duo as entertaining as Bob Culp and Bill Cosby on "I Spy."

Kato is played by a 25-year-old Chinese, Bruce Lee, and he's bright and funny—as well as an expert on Oriental fighting. He was in Minneapolis over the weekend as a guest of KMSP, which will run ABC's Hornet program come fall.

I asked Lee about the cliché image most of us have of Oriental self-defense—the technique that supposedly enables a 90-pound woman to toss a 250-pound assailant. His answer:

"Let us put it this way: 99 percent of the whole business of Oriental self-defense is baloney. It's fancy jazz. It looks good, but it doesn't work. If that 90-pound woman is attacked, the only thing she can do is strike hard at one of three places—the eye-balls, the groin or the shins. This should be sufficient to put the man off-balance for just a moment, and then she'd better run like hell."

That sort of disdain for judo, karate, etc., comes as even more of a surprise when you learn that in addition to acting, Lee runs three schools on the West Coast, all teaching that sort of thing.

I say that if you want something beautiful, take modern dancing. What good would it do a boxer to learn to meditate? He's a fighter, not a monk. It's all too ritualistic, what with bowing and posturing. That sort of Oriental self-defense is like swimming on land. You can learn all the swimming strokes, but if you're never in the water, it's nonsense. These guys never fight. They all want to break three-inch boards or two bricks or something. Why? That doesn't make them fighters.

Who comes to them? He replies, "People from every walk of life. Some want to lose weight. Some say they want to be able to defend themselves. But I would say that the majority are there for one reason—vanity. It is exotic. They figure they'll learn Zen and meditation.

"I say that if you want something beautiful, take modern dancing. What good would it do a boxer to learn to meditate? He's a fighter, not a monk. It's all too ritualistic, what with bowing and posturing. That sort of Oriental self-defense is like swimming on land. You can learn all the swimming strokes, but if you're never in the water, it's nonsense. These guys never fight. They all want to break three-inch boards or two bricks or something. Why? That doesn't make them fighters."

Lee's Particular Specialty is called Gung-Fu. His explanation of it is that it is deadly simplicity. It's a matter of hitting fast and deadly. "I'm 140 pounds," he says, "and if I don't get my opponent in three blows, I'm through. I use my hands and my feet, and it is done so swiftly that I've had to slow down so the cameras can catch the action. I saw the first takes, and it just looked like people were falling down—no one could see me strike them."

I asked if there was any danger that the kids viewing would imitate this stuff. "I doubt it," Lee replied. "However the producer did ask me to kick a little higher."

On the show, Lee will be the silent type. Which is a shame, he says, because he told the producer: "how lucky can you get—you've got a Chinaman from Hong Kong who can say 'Britt Reid.'" (That's the Hornet's name.)

Lee has been in show business since he was six, when he was in Chinese movies. His father was in the Chinese opera, which Lee describes as "gongs and the whole bit—I had a heck of a time understanding what was going on." He came to the U.S. in 1959, met his future wife at the University of Washington, and now has a blond, gray-eyed son.

Naturally the offering is jokingly called Number One Son. "Just at the time he was born," Lee says, "I appeared at a karate competition in Long Beach, and William Dozier (producer) offered me the lead in a series titled "Number One Son," about Charlie Chan's son, a sort of Chinese James Bond. It was all set to go, and then Batman became a hit, so Dozier got me into this Green Hornet bit."

Chicago's American, August 23, 1966

HORNET'S SIDEKICK A BLUR ON FILM

by Bill Irvin

We have some advice for the Green Hornet's foes. Before you tangle with him, take a good look at the young fellow who is usually at his side.

His name is Kato—and before you can say Kato he'll kick you back into January—1902, that is.

Kato is a two-legged deadly weapon, a master of Gung-Fu, the oriental art of self-defense.

The American-born Chinese actor, whose professional name is Bruce Lee, got his role in "The Green Hornet"—premiering on ABC-TV, Friday, Sept. 9—without even a screen test.[45]

Bill Dozier, producer of ABC's "Batman" series, saw Bruce performing in a world karate tournament and signed him for a projected TV show called, "Number One Son," son of Charlie Chan, a sort of Chinese James Bond.

Just about the time Dozier got involved in "Batman," who fast became his Number One Son on television.

Bruce was still under contract and when "The Green Hornet" got the big buzz from ABC, there was no question in Producer Dozier's mind who would play the Hornet's sidekick, Kato.

When the Hornet (Van Williams) gets in a jam, Kato is nearby to clobber his enemies. He strikes with such lightning speed that he makes a rattler look like a study in slow motion.

He was so fast in one fight scene in the opening show that it had to be shot over. "It was just a blur on film," says Bruce. "Gung-Fu is going to be the big thing in 'The Green Hornet.' They are going to portray me as The Weapon. I will be handling most of the fighting. When we first started shooting the series, everybody thought I was putting them on with the name Gung-Fu. But it is a legitimate system of self-defense. In fact, it is the oldest. There are other branches, like karate, judo, and ju-jitsu, which have either derived from Gung-Fu or have been influenced by it. Gung-Fu is more offensive than defensive. At the moment of attack, you intercept the attack and attack in return."

Bruce was born in San Francisco but went to Hong Kong with his family when he was three-months old. His father was a producer of Chinese opera.[46]

"When I was 13, I was kind of a juvenile delinquent in Hong Kong and got into a lot of fights in which I learned about Gung-Fu," says Bruce. "The more I learned about Gung-Fu, the more I liked it. Then I went to a special school and trained myself. Later on, I helped teach in the school. When I came to the United States in 1959, I opened a Gung-Fu school of my own in Seattle and another one in Oakland.

"One of the main characteristics of 'The Green Hornet' show will be the speed of the fights and the simplicity in finishing off the Hornet's enemies. I try to maintain as much speed as I can although I have to keep telling myself 'Slow down, slow down,' so the cameras can catch the action."

Bruce has a percentage of "The Green Hornet" merchandising rights, and if the show catches on there will surely be a Green Hornet film feature, just as Batman spawned a movie based on the TV series.[47]

A successful Green Hornet series also probably will mean a national Gung-Fu craze among the small fry, who may be expected to go around kicking the daylights out of one another.

There also will be all sorts of Gung-Fu merchandise. Gung-Fu bubble gum is ready for the market.

So, just let the Green Hornet's foes beware. They'll find themselves bashed in as though they had been kicked by 10 mules if Kato gets a crack at them.

Seattle Post-Intelligencer (sports section), December 31, 1966

WHAT'S THAT BUZZING?

by John Owen

It's difficult to argue with the selection of the remarkable Eddie Cotton as Seattle's Man of the Year in Sports. But if the members of the tribunal had known Kato was in town…Well, you'd have to believe he'd have received a few written votes.

It's true that Cotton has met some pretty tough characters this past year—guys like Jose Torres and Roger Rouse. But Kato hasn't exactly been resting on his haunches, either.

"He tried to draw a gun on me," Kato recalls. "So, PLEW, I threw a dart at him, then BLAM-BLAM-BLAM-BLAM, and it was all over."

Even more spectacular, was the match with another Gung-Fu expert named Low Sing.[48] "Oh, we had a big fight. I got a little scratch up here on my head, but I finally won." Unlike Cotton, Kato did not have to wait around for the judges' verdict. "I killed him," Kato explains, modestly. In boxing, this is known as a unanimous decision.

You won't find Kato listed in [the] Ring Record Book, but ABC-TV press agents explain that he is "Britt Reid's faithful companion and aide in 'The Green Hornet,' who often steps in to save the Green Hornet when they are battling criminals."

This is putting it mildly. It's probably safe to say that were it not for Kato, the Green Hornet would be walking around today with a bent stinger.

But under the Mask...

In real life, however, Kato is really Bruce Lee—a native of Hong Kong, a former student at the University of Washington, a holiday visitor in Seattle and an extremely agreeable and articulate guy.

When you meet him in real life, you realize that he's only about 5-8, maybe 140 or 150 pounds. Can you imagine what would happen if a little guy like that really came up against Big Dan Carley? I'll tell you what would happen:

PLEW! Also BLAM-BLAM-BLAM-BLAM! In that order. And Big Dan would be sitting in the corner on his ear.

You see, Lee is also a $30 an hour instructor in Gung-Fu, an Oriental method of self-defense. And if you think that this is just a press agent's dream, Bruce would probably be happy to kick you in the groin by way of introduction. In fact, he had never acted until someone from 20th Century-Fox saw him give a demonstration of

Gung-Fu in 1964 at the World Karate Championships in Long Beach.[49]

Lee differs from many such instructors, who feel you must execute the proper ritualistic moves, and utter some impressive guttural chants before kicking an acquaintance in the teeth. Lee teaches his pupils how to deliver a kick to the teeth in the quickest and simplest possible manner. If they want to genuflect and grunt afterward, that's their option.

"Ninety per cent of Oriental self defense is baloney…it's organized despair," Lee says. "I teach the Jun Fan Method.[50] I stress simplicity, directness and non-classical instruction. It isn't ritual and it isn't sport. It's self defense."

It is also, obviously, bad news to anyone on the receiving end. Lee's arsenal is an impressive one, even to an observer seated a safe 10 feet away.

Biff, Bam and Etc.

"At long range, you use a kick to the shins in the same way a boxer uses his left jab. At closer range, you use a finger jab to the eyes or throat. Even closer, you employ a curved arm blow to the head, the ribs or the solar plexus. When you're in a clinch you use your elbow, knee and the instep kick."

To demonstrate, Lee delivered a furious volley of kicks and punches at an obliging friend and local instructor named Taky Kimura. Each blow or kick would have stretched Kimura out on the floor. Yet each lightning-quick blow and kick ended just an inch away from Kimura's head.

For a parting demonstration, Lee placed a dime in the upturned palm of a reporter. Little did he know that the reporter possessed hair-trigger reflexes from long association with athletes and athletics.

"I'm going to try to pick that dime out of your palm. Don't let me do it," Lee cautioned.

His fingers poised above the upturned palm, then suddenly he grabbed. He was too slow. The sportswriter's fist closed with the speed of a steel trap. "Hey," Lee marveled, "you've got pretty fast reflexes." The reporter blushed becomingly. "Let me see that dime," Lee asked. The reporter opened his fist. In his palm was a penny. Lee was holding the dime. Boy, I'm telling you, Green Hornet. Just be glad he's on your side!

Newspaper article entitled "Man Alive"

(source unknown, ca. 1966)

THE LOST VENERATION

by Bill Fiset

Wild bit in San Leandro: Bruce Lee, the Gung-Fu expert who hit it big in Hollywood playing "Kato" on "The Green Hornet" TV show, called and made a quiet appointment with Dr. Jim Durkin, the optometrist, because Lee wanted contact lenses. Durkin made the mistake of telling his young daughters, seventh and eighth graders at Assumption School, that the Chinese actor was coming in. So Lee showed up for his eye examination. What did he see on the chart? About 20 little girls, all jammed in the office.

Seattle newspaper, ca. 1966

Vivian McCulloch's son-in-law, Bruce Lee, who is Kato on the "Green Hornet" series on TV, made a visit to our office to have coffee with Vivian.[51] He was swamped for autograph requests from the girls. Even our boss, Mr. MacDonald, received one for his children who are avid fans.

Notes

1. Lee was only three months old—not three years old—when his family returned to Hong Kong.

2. Gung fu is not a sport and Bruce Lee certainly never considered it to be one. Its concerns are self-defense and self-mastery. During his lifetime, Bruce Lee wrote only one book, entitled *Chinese Gung Fu: The Philosophical Art of Self-Defense,* which he self-published in 1963 (reissued in 1987 by Ohara Publications). He had, however, been working on a second, more substantial work, *The Tao of Gung Fu* (Charles E. Tuttle Co.).

3. While there is evidence that Burt Ward was once a student of karate, he was by no means an expert. In fact, Van Williams related to this editor, during a phone conversation in 1993, that Ward's claim that he was an expert in the martial arts upset Bruce Lee considerably. According to Williams:

> Bruce didn't like karate. He got a lot of people in karate turned off against him because he didn't believe in all that black belt, yellow belt, red belt, and the degrees, and the way that they did it. Nevertheless, while he may have thought that the art had its shortcomings, he still held a great respect for those individuals who went through all the discipline necessary to earn their belts—whatever the color happened to be. I mean, most of his friends were martial artists from all sorts of disciplines because he, deep-down, felt an affinity with them; that, at some level, they were all searching for a "better way" to advance the arts. And, for this reason, he absolutely hated phonies, people who claimed that they were black belts when, in fact, they weren't.

> I happened to witness Bruce's encounter with an individual who claimed to be a black belt once on the set of "The Green Hornet." What happened was that the producers of "The Green Hornet" wanted to somehow get us on "Batman" to try and pick up some of Batman's audience. And the shows weren't compatible. We played it straight—we were bound and determined to play it straight—and they were camping it up all over the place with "WHIP! WHAM! BAM!" So, they had a deal in the original script that we get into a fracas with Batman and Robin—and lose—because it was their show. Bruce walked off the set. He said "There's no way that I'm going to get into a fight with Robin and lose. That makes me look like an idiot!" So they pacified him and I think we all ended up in a "draw." I don't even remember but I think they called it the "crossover," like some sort of religious experience or something. Well, we "crossed over" to that show, and did it, and made fools of ourselves, and then went back to our deal.

> But Bruce supposedly just intimidated the hell out of Robin. In other words, Bruce agreed to the "draw," but he was going to show Robin. You know all that Chinese huffing and puffing and all of the stuff they do in the

martial arts? Well, evidently Robin was just scared shitless. I mean he was so goddamned afraid that Bruce was going to tie into him over that and he had all these guys watching and going to protect him if Bruce got mad and got into it. So I think he was really shaking in his boots. Burt Ward had claimed that he was a black belt. (I think he might have worn one once in his life but I don't think he ever learned one damn thing.) Anyway, he had gone around, because Bruce was very popular with the kids, and they were starting to ask Robin "Can you do that thing that Bruce does?" And Robin would say "Oh, yeah, well I'm a black belt, watch this: EEW-WHA-HA!" and he'd do his little stance, which was a joke.

When Bruce and he finally got together, he was really quaking in his boots. He really thought Bruce was going to light into him—and Bruce made everybody think that. He told everybody on the set that he was going to tie into this guy and "show him how it was really done and then we'll see how great a black belt you are, boy!" It was hard to keep a straight face looking at Robin. I was just watching all that stuff; Bruce was stern, not joking—which is not Bruce; he was always joking and playing around on the set. But, boy, he came swaggering on that set! And he was staring him down and everything else. I'm telling you he had him scared to death!

There is evidence from Bruce Lee's daytimer diary that Burt Ward completed only one lesson under his instruction, which took place on Wednesday, May 25, 1966.
4. Bruce Lee held no use for martial arts tournaments which, in his day, were all noncontact affairs called "point karate." He had no desire to compete in such tournaments, which he considered primarily to be "games of protecting one's ego."
5. This statement is false, possibly created by the author of the piece to capitalize on the recognition of the better-known (in North America) martial art of karate. Bruce Lee was never a student of karate, although he was very knowledgeable about that art and its varied techniques. In fact, many black belts and world champions in karate, such as Chuck Norris, came to Bruce Lee for instruction throughout the course of Lee's lifetime.
6. Linda Emery was born in Everett, Washington—not Seattle. Her religious upbringing was a combination of Baptist and Presbyterian.
7. Linda actually was a pre-med student.
8. Grace Lee, Bruce Lee's mother, was one-fourth German—not British.
9. Bruce Lee was actually enrolled in a Catholic school, where he was taught by Chinese headmasters. He did not attend a "British private school."
10. Bruce Lee obtained his American high school diploma from Edison Technical School in Seattle.
11. As Bruce Lee only spoke two languages fluently—English and Cantonese—it is doubtful that he taught classes in the Mandarin dialect. It is more likely that he taught classes in his mother tongue, Cantonese, or more likely still that he taught gung fu and/or Chinese philosophy.
12. Linda Emery's "auditing language lessons" is a fabrication. Linda met Bruce Lee when she attended his gung fu class.

13. This is not true. In fact, according to Linda, "Bruce was the only person from Hong Kong that I knew."

14. Linda has stated that this sentence is a complete fabrication: "We didn't know anybody who lived at the beach and water sports were never part of our weekend activities." She further queried: "What's a splash party?"

15. According to Linda, this is not quite the way the subject of their first date was broached. During a gung fu class, Bruce had tackled Linda while demonstrating a move in the big courtyard near The Columns on the University of Washington campus. Bruce asked Linda, "Do you want to go out to dinner with me tonight?"

Looking around at the small class, Linda replied, "You mean all of us?"

"No," Bruce answered, "Just you."

16. This scenario "never happened" says Linda Lee Cadwell.

17. Again, Linda, says that no such conversation ever took place. In fact, Linda did not discuss the subject of her marrying Bruce until she was confronted with it by her family.

> It was a surprise to them when I said that we were going to get married. Actually we were going to run away and get married, but in the state of Washington, when you apply for a marriage license, they publish it in the newspaper. Well, being eighteen or nineteen years old, I didn't know that. I guess that one of my maiden aunties didn't have too much to do that day, so she was reading the vital statistics in the newspaper and saw that "a Linda Emery was going to marry a Bruce Jun Fan Lee" and called my mother and told her that. So it all came out on the table at that point, which, in retrospect, was the best thing. So there was a family powwow and aunts and uncles came over and everyone tried to dissuade me from doing this. I know they had our best interests at heart, and so I have no bad feelings about that time, but it was difficult for everyone.

> I just have to say, though, that there are very few times in one's life when you absolutely know for certain that you are doing the right thing and that this was one of those times. This was a man of quality, and integrity, and great love, and warmth. [I knew] that we were going to be okay. So we did get married, and my mother did attend the wedding.

18. Although Bruce Lee's father was well-travelled, it would be technically inaccurate to call him a "true cosmopolite." He was very proud of being Chinese, and would have considered himself as such.

19. Bruce and Linda Lee were married on August 17, 1964—not March 17, 1964.

20. Linda wore a sleeveless, brown, floral dress—not a sleeveless white dress. The wedding ring Bruce gave to Linda was actually one he had borrowed from his friend, and assistant–gung fu instructor, James Yimm Lee.

21. Taky Kimura remained one of Bruce Lee's closest friends throughout Lee's lifetime. He not only provided a more seasoned sounding board off which Bruce would bounce his many ideas, but he was also Lee's assistant instructor of gung fu in Seattle. Kimura remains a very humble, decent, and kind human being, who is purely genuine in both word and deed.

22. Bruce and Linda moved to Oakland, California, immediately after they were married. There, they lived at the house of Lee's close friend and assistant instructor, James Yimm Lee. They did not "rent an apartment."

23. It was actually the other way around: Bruce Lee appeared at a karate tournament in Long Beach, where he gave a demonstration of the Chinese art of gung fu.

24. Lee was not placed under a five-year contract, but rather received a one-year retainer in the amount of $1,800.

25. Brandon Bruce Lee was born on February 1, 1965, in Oakland, California. He had a middle name—his father's English given name, Bruce.

26. Bruce Lee's father, Lee Hoi Chuen, passed away one week after the birth of Brandon, on February 8, 1965, in Hong Kong.

27. "This definitely never happened," Linda Lee Cadwell comments.

28. In truth, Linda did not receive her wedding rings until years later.

29. Another example of poetic license. "I never burst into tears upon hearing firecrackers in Hong Kong," Linda recalls. "This little anecdote never happened. Hong Kong was all new and exciting to me and I was simply happy to be experiencing it with my husband and son."

30. While it might be called Zen, it would be more accurate to say that the philosophical influence on Chinese gung fu is decidedly Buddhist or Taoist, in the form of Ch'an. Zen is actually a Japanese word derived from the Chinese Ch'an or Ch'an-na, which are, in turn, forms of the Sanskrit dhyana—typically rendered as "meditation" or "contemplation" in English. However, this does not do the term full justice. It is more closely allied to the Greek gnosis, or "knowledge," in the sense of supreme spiritual enlightenment.

31. This was exactly how Brandon Lee's education unfolded. He did indeed attend an American school—Emerson College in Boston, Massachusetts—and he also received a portion of his grade school education in Hong Kong, where he even attended, for a time, the same grade school as his father.

32. The phrase "walk on" was an important one in Bruce Lee's philosophy. He even had it written on the back of one of his business cards, which he displayed on his desk to remind himself to walk on, or flow on, in the current of life. One time, when Taky Kimura had experienced an emotional upset, Bruce wrote him a poignant letter indicating: "Life is an ever-flowing process and somewhere on the path some unpleasant things will pop up—it might leave a scar—but then life is flowing on, and like running water, when it stops, it grows stale. Go bravely on, my friend, because each experience teaches us a lesson."

33. This would prove to be a key principle in Lee's philosophy of life—look at all things and draw from them the essence that made for their effectiveness—as well as being the cornerstone of his martial philosophy of Jun Fan jeet kune do.

34. Bruce Lee was asked to appear at the 1964 International Karate Tournament to demonstrate the art of Chinese gung fu—not because he was "good at karate."

35. Gung fu is not "an Oriental off-shoot of karate and judo," but rather the forerunner, by several thousand years, of these arts.

36. This reads as though Taky Kimura would be operating the Los Angeles school, which was not the case. Lee had Kimura remain in Seattle, where he ran the Seattle

branch of the Jun Fan Gung Fu Institute. The Los Angeles branch was presided over by Lee himself and, in his absence, by Daniel Inosanto, Lee's assistant instructor.

37. Lee returned to Hong Kong in 1963 (the first time since leaving in 1959), but for only three months. Rather than spending "most of last year" (1965) in Hong Kong, Lee then returned for only four months.

38. Lee was probably misquoted. Bruce Lee never had his own gung fu school in Hong Kong. He did, however, have schools in Seattle and Oakland and, within a year, would have a third school in Los Angeles. However, the school where he was first taught the fundamentals of Wing Chun gung fu was still operating in Hong Kong at the time this article was written.

39. Bruce Lee did not "compete" at the 1964 Long Beach International Karate Championship, but rather demonstrated the art of gung fu. It is important to recognize that in the 1960s so-called karate tournaments were noncontact affairs, not to be confused with full-contact martial arts like Thai kickboxing or Western boxing. Consequently, Bruce Lee wanted nothing to do with their tournaments, which he viewed as having as much to do with real combat as games of tag. While the champions of karate tournaments were winning their noncontact titles, Bruce Lee was busy creating new ways to make his martial art training more realistic; these included elements such as full-contact sparring.

40. Footage of Lee's demonstration—not the karate matches—sold Dozier on casting Bruce Lee in "Number One Son."

41. A reference to the popular "I Spy" TV series that aired in the 1960s starring Bill Cosby and Robert Culp. Lee had genuinely hoped to be portrayed as an equal on the series as opposed to the manservant, not for more camera time, but rather to assert the dignity of the Chinese. To this end, on June 21, 1966, a mere 15 days after "The Green Hornet" began production, Bruce Lee penned the following letter to William Dozier, executive producer of the series:

> Dear Mr. Dozier:
>
> Simplicity—to express the utmost in the minimum of lines and energy—is the goal of gung fu, and acting is not too much different. Since the first episode, I've gained actual experience. I've learned to be "simply human" without unnecessary striving. I believe in Kato and am truthfully justifying the physical actions [of the character] economically.
>
> Actually, what I like to express here is regarding the relationship between the Green Hornet and Kato. True that Kato is a house boy of Britt [Reid] but as the crime fighter, Kato is an "active partner" of the Green Hornet and not a "mute follower." Jeff Corey [Lee's acting coach at Twentieth Century-Fox] agrees and I myself feel that at least an occasional dialogue would certainly make me "feel" more at home with the fellow players. It does take a real pro to just stand there in big close up. I've learned the effectiveness of simplicity but in order to cultivate simplicity, something to say or do is necessary...from firmness comes gentleness, and complexity leads to simplicity. However, alone standing there apart from the fellow

players listening is itself simplicity stripped to the very end. That requires considerable skill because it is simple!

I've presented two scripts to Jeff Corey, but so far we've been doing other exercises because there just isn't anything in the script to work on.

I'm not complaining, but I feel that an "active partnership" with the Green Hornet will definitely bring out a more effective and efficient Kato. My aim is for the betterment of the show and I bother you with this because you have been most understanding.

42. Bruce Lee's major at the University of Washington was philosophy, not drama or arts and sciences.

43. Bruce Lee left the University of Washington not to fight crime for television, but to get married and to open a gung fu school in Oakland. It was after his appearance at the Long Beach International Karate Championships that Lee first became involved in television. "The Green Hornet" series didn't begin filming until June 1966.

44. While it's true that Bruce Lee won a cha-cha championship, the title and year are incorrect. The title was Crown Colony Cha-Cha Championship, which Lee won in 1958. He maintained his interest in dancing throughout his life, buying books and subscribing to magazines on the subject. Further, Lee kept a list of 108 different cha-cha steps in his wallet.

45. This is not true. Bruce Lee sat for a screen test for Twentieth Century-Fox in 1965, when they were considering him for a lead role in "Number One Son."

46. Bruce Lee's father was never a "producer of Chinese Opera"; he was a well-known actor in the Chinese opera.

47. False. Linda Lee Cadwell denies that Bruce ever had a stake in the merchandising rights of "The Green Hornet."

48. From the episode of "The Green Hornet" entitled "The Praying Mantis," which dealt extensively with gung fu, allowing Bruce Lee to showcase his skills in the art. The part of Low Sing was played by veteran actor Mako (except for the gung fu fighting scenes in which he was doubled by Bruce Lee's real-life student, Daniel Inosanto).

49. By the time Bruce Lee arrived in the United States at age eighteen, he had appeared in some twenty feature films in Hong Kong, mostly in co-starring roles. (See "Chronological List of Bruce Lee's Principal Works," pages 17–19, for more details.)

50. Jun Fan was Bruce Lee's Chinese first, or given, name. Translated literally, "Jun Fan" means "to arouse and shake the foreign countries." When Lee opened his first formal gung fu school in Seattle, he called it the Jun Fan Gung Fu Institute.

51. Bruce Lee was not a coffee drinker—tea, perhaps.

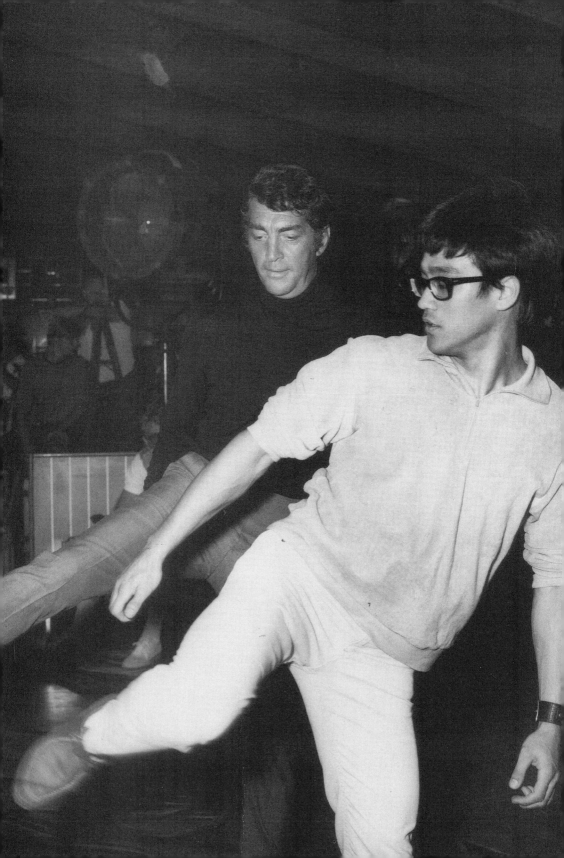

Part 3

THE
HOLLYWOOD
YEARS

(1967–1970)

The Washington Post, May 1967[1]*

KATO LIKES PUNS, PREYS ON WORDS

by Willard Clopton Jr.

"They were very lucky to get me," remarked Bruce Lee. "After all, how many Chinese can pronounce Britt Reid?" Lee, who was raised in Hong Kong, plays Kato on "The Green Hornet," the weekly adventure series now living out its first and last season on ABC-TV.

Lee was bluntly analytical about the production's demise. In the first place, he said, it was far enough out, not Batmanish enough to please the viewers. Second it should have been an hour-length show. "Besides," he added, "the scripts were lousy."

Bruce Lee did not believe in the "belt system," such as those used by karate instructors, believing that the motivation for meaningful improvement results not from external trinkets, but rather within the will of each individual.

Got the Hint

He got a hint of the show's shaky status a few months ago, in a letter from a network executive. "He wrote to say that although the show had not been renewed, this did not mean it was going off the air. Then he added that he had enjoyed working with me. A little later I got a note from the executive producer, Bill Dozier, that said: 'Confucius say, Green Hornet to buzz no more.'"

Besides his acting, Lee, 26, is a master of the two-finger pushup, connoisseur of bad puns ("700 million Chinese can't all be Wong") and an expert at kung fu, a Chinese

---

*Notes to Part 3 begin on page 100.

forerunner of karate. "I possess the yellow belt. It signifies that I can run pretty damn fast."

His proficiency at kung fu is the reason he is in Washington. He will give a demonstration tonight as part of the Third Annual National Karate Championship, being staged at the National Guard Armory by the Korean Cultural and Freedom Foundation.

I possess the yellow belt. It signifies that I can run pretty damn fast.

It is a hopped-up adaptation of "The Green Hornet" that ABC is presenting.

The original radio version, in the 1930s, dealt with the exploits of a crusading newspaper publisher, Britt Reid, and his Japanese houseboy, Kato.

Today's Reid, played by actor Van Williams, has branched out to acquire a TV station and a miniskirted secretary. Kato, who suddenly became a Filipino houseboy on Dec. 8, 1941, is now depicted as vaguely oriental, with no specific land of origin.

Lee likes to make jokes about his Chinese ancestry. Lunching with newsmen yesterday, he was brought a bowl of soup and asked: "Now how in hell am I supposed to eat this with chopsticks?"

He was actually born in San Francisco, where his father was touring with a native Chinese opera company.

Three weeks later he was returned to Hong Kong, where he lived until he was 18.[2] Then he came back to this country to study philosophy and psychology at the University of Washington.

Three years ago, he gave a kung fu demonstration at Long Beach, Calif. A film executive caught the act, one thing led to another and Lee wound up with the part of Kato.[3]

Lee is being considered for roles in two new dramatic series. "One is a one-hour fantasy—that's all I can say. The other is a kind of 'I Spy' thing called 'Charlie and Chan.' I'd be Charlie, a kung fu teacher, and Chan would be a ski instructor."

Lee and his Caucasian wife are parents of a 2-year-old son "who must be the world's only blonde-haired Chinaman."

Lee boasts that "I don't smoke, don't drink and don't gamble, but that's as far as I go. I do chew gum. After all, many men smoke, but fu manchu."

Springfield Union News, July 5, 1967

GUNG FU IS SERIOUS BUSINESS TO KATO, THE GREEN HORNET'S MUSCULAR AID

Dressed in black, with boots and hair to match, at first sight Bruce Lee, better known as "Kato" of television's "The Green Hornet," looks menacing.

During demonstrations of the ancient Chinese art of Gung Fu, the art of self-defense which is the ancestor of karate and judo, Lee thrilled three audiences at Riverside Park Tuesday with his physical skills.

However, talking with him between shows, Lee displayed an engaging charm while describing life in China, his native Hong Kong and, alas, Hollywood.

"I couldn't live by a rigid schedule. I try to live freely from moment to moment, letting things happen and adjusting to them."

Well spoken, with dark, fluttering eyes, the 25-year-old son of a Chinese Opera star, Lee demonstrated the physical benefits of his studies into Gung Fu by doing push-ups on two-fingers of one hand, and on his two thumbs. "Gung Fu is not like the comic books who promise they can make a hero out of you in three weeks. It's a way of life."

Lee studied at the University of Washington where he met his wife. The study of philosophy led to his writing many books on Gung Fu. "Gung Fu means an empty mind. Not just thinking about nothingness, which still implies thinking."

Speaking more like a sage than a hornet, he said, "Everything has two parts which make one whole. In Gung Fu there is always give and take, and the understanding of the whole picture is the important thing."

He said the "fluidity" a Gung Fu student seeks can best be described by the story of the centipede. The many-footed creature was asked how it managed to walk on all its feet. When it stopped to think about how it managed its daily function, it tripped and fell. And so, life should be a natural process, in which the development of the mind is not allowed to throw the natural flow of life out of balance.

Lee says he plans to stay in the United States. "In the Orient there is too much smiling and turning the other cheek, until your back is turned. Here people say what they think right away. Also, the opportunities here are limitless. Everyone has their own house and car, even though they spend the rest of their lives paying for it."

"In Hong Kong, a high school graduate might go to work in a bank or for the government, but there is little scope for improvement." He said Hong Kong is tightly sealed off from the mainland of China. Talking about the Red Guard and recent revolts in China he said, "China was so desperately in need of some great changes that communism is doing some good for the people. The great danger is in the nuclear bomb."

Asked about China's hostility he said, "Like any poor country or person they are hostile while they are down. If you have nothing, you can afford to be hostile. But wait until they, too, become more prosperous. They will soon quiet down and want peace just like the rest of the world."

Since "The Green Hornet" is no longer in production, Lee will continue his tours until a new series comes along. He also owns

Gung Fu gymnasiums. Assisting Lee in his demonstrations was John Quinn of the Springfield YMCA. Henry Jay of the Holyoke YMCA helped make arrangements for the demonstrations.

The Seattle Times, 1967[4]

GUNG FU IN BRIDGE CLUB?

Yep, Beats Shin-Kicking

by Don Duncan

Millions of television watchers this past season knew him as Kato, scourge of the underworld in the now defunct The Green Hornet series.

But he dazzled a crowd in the Roanoke Bridge Club the other night as plain Bruce Lee, master of the Chinese art of mayhem, Gung Fu. Gung Fu in a bridge club? Well now, you must admit a mere kick of your bridge partner's shins sometimes does not express the true intensity of your feelings. Gung Fu the idiot!

Gung Fu is a cross between Thai boxing and back-alley brawling. None of this stylized karate stuff. The object of Gung Fu is to send a foe to the nearest hospital in the shortest possible time, what Lee calls "a maximum of anguish with a minimum of movement." The direct approach.

This is accomplished with knees, elbows, fingers in the eyes, feet in the teeth. Lee delivers these blows so fast they are almost a blur. Lee claims 5 feet 8 inches and 145 pounds, but looks two inches shorter than that. Yet those who watched him would bet on Lee to render Cassius Clay senseless if they were put in a room and told that anything goes.

Born in San Francisco, Lee was whisked off to Hong Kong with his parents when he was 3 months old. His father was a featured performer in Chinese Opera. Lee early learned the grease-paint routine.

When he returned to this country in 1959, he studied philosophy at the University of Washington. He met and married Linda McCulloch, a graduate of Garfield High School.[5]

Or this matter of breaking bricks and boards with the edge of your hand. Now I ask you, did you ever see a brick or a board pick a fight with anybody? This is gimmick stuff. A human being doesn't just stand there and wait to be hit.

The Lees were in town to visit Linda's parents, Mr. and Mrs. David McCulloch. They have a son, Brandon, 2½, whom Lee calls "the only blue-eyed, blond Chinese in the world."

When he isn't playing the cold-eyed Kato, Lee is the complete ham, alternately the pixie and the tough kid down the block. He puns unmercifully, performs dazzling feats of speed and coordination, wades bravely into the rip-tides of a language he is trying to master.

Sample Lee wit:

"Seven hundred million Chinese can't be Wong."

"I don't drink or smoke. But I do chew gum, because fu man chu."

Lee stunts:

One-armed pushups, using only the thumb and forefinger.

Having a man from the crowd, proud of his reflexes, hold a dime in the palm of his outstretched hand. Lee, his hand hovering a foot above the outstretched hand, proceeds to remove the dime and leave a penny—before the other can clench his fist.

Lee came to the attention of the television world when he lectured at the 1964 World Karate Championships. A spectator, with television connections, thought Lee had the "greatest natural acting ability" he had ever seen.

Without even taking a screen test, Lee was booked for a series to be called "Number One Son," based loosely on the old Charlie

Chan yarns. The series didn't get off the typewriter. Up popped the role of Kato, originally written for a Japanese. Lee didn't mind.

With "The Green Hornet" having buzzed off to the hive where Nielsen failures go, Lee is now in line for an "I Spy"–type series set in Hawaii, a super-C.I.A. thing in which he would be paired with a Caucasian sleuth. "You might say," Lee said, "that I'll be an Oriental Bill Cosby."

Just back from the 1967 Karate Championships, Lee is mildly critical of this time-honored art of "self-defense."

"There's so much myth and baloney," Lee says. "Like a 90-year-old man able to manhandle a 300-pounder with his little finger. Ridiculous. Or this matter of breaking bricks and boards with the edge of your hand. Now I ask you, did you ever see a brick or a board pick a fight with anybody? This is gimmick stuff. A human being doesn't just stand there and wait to be hit."

Lee says many students of karate are so wrapped up in the snorting sounds and the counter moves that they lose sight of what they should be doing to an opponent—"get him out of there, quick."

"The karate teacher says, 'if your opponent does this, then you do this, and then you do this and then you do this.' And while you are remembering the 'and thens' the other guy is killing you. Gung Fu has been stripped to a minimum of fancy stuff. Clean and simple destruction. Your opponent is at a distance, kick him in the groin. He gets close, poke him in the eye, bring up your knee, pop him with an elbow, dig a corkscrew punch to his stomach. Faced with the choice of socking your opponent in the head or poking him in the eyes, you go for the eyes every time," Lee says.

"Sure, it's a little like Thai boxing, except that if you had a Gung Fu fight, there'd never be any round three. Somebody would be lying on the floor."

Lee started Gung Fu at age 13. At age 26 he still isn't as large as many American junior-high boys. But he is enormously strong.

Three Bruce Lee Gung Fu schools have been set up on the

Pacific Coast—Los Angeles, San Francisco and at 420 B Eighth Ave. S., where Taky Kimura is the sifu (teacher).[6]

The Gung Fu movement is strictly gung ho these days.

Charlotte, North Carolina, newspaper, October 24, 1969

JUDO EXPERT CALLS HAND CHOP "STUNT"

by Emery Wister

Bruce Lee can break a six-inch board with one karate blow of his callused hand, but shucks, he'd just as soon not. "Just a stunt," snorts the expert on what he calls the Oriental martial arts. "How many times have you seen a board hitting you back? Now breaking a neck, well, that's more concrete."

The main thing is teaching a man to do his thing, just be himself. The individual is more important than style.

Lee, who played the wiry Kato in the television series "The Green Hornet" a few years ago, was in Charlotte yesterday to promote the new motion picture *Marlowe*. The movie, starring James Garner as Philip Chandler's famed private eye, casts Lee as a Chinese gangster who kills his victims by karate. It comes to the Park Terrace Friday.

"Karate, judo, aikido, I teach them all," says Lee who has his "clubs" in Los Angeles, Oakland and Seattle.[7] "I charge my students $500 for a 10 lesson course. But it takes a man at least 18 months to become proficient at it."

And how does a person learn karate or any of the other defensive arts? Why, by being himself. "The main thing is teaching a man to do his thing, just be himself. The individual is more important than style. If a person is awkward he should not try to be agile. I'm against trying to impose a style on a man. This is an art, an expression of a man's own self." Anyway, after 10, 45-minute sessions the student has learned something, enough, he says, "to kick and run like hell."

"We have a lot more men than women studying the defensive arts now. In fact, I don't have any women at all at the moment.

A billboard announcing Bruce Lee's appearance, not as a martial artist but as a "noted agilist (sic)" during a promotional tour that Lee did in October of 1969 to promote his role in the movie "Marlowe."

Women couldn't compete with men at this, anyway. I don't care what you've heard, there's no such thing as a 90-pound weakling tossing a 250-pound giant."

Lee who gives a one-man demonstration of how to wreck an office in *Marlowe*, is a reasonably short, well-built man. He's a native of Hong Kong and has worked his karate magic on a number of television shows.

"I don't chop," he says describing his technique. "If I raise my hands to my shoulders I'll get several jabs from my opponent before I can get my arms down. For practice I would prefer trying to break a board hanging in a vertical position. I can break one from eight to 10 inches thick."

To see Lee's hands is to believe this. They are hard as pine. His knuckles are capped with calluses as hard as pine knots themselves. "There's a secret in breaking a board with a karate chop," he said. "You have to go with the grain. If you condition yourself well enough and concentrate it will break."

Next spring or summer Lee will produce and play a featured role in a movie on the Oriental martial arts. The popular star James Coburn, who had done a little karate fighting himself in pictures, will play the lead.

KARATE IS SISSY STUFF

Kids, if you're wondering if the Green Hornet's main man Kato is really a top-notch karate expert, the answer is yes.[8]

He's just a little guy, but he's fast like greased lightning and pretty smart upstairs too. Kato was in town recently as he was touring the Carolinas. His real name is Bruce Lee; he was born in Hong Kong 28 years ago.

One newsman wanted to know if he could break boards with a chop. "I don't chop, that's sissy stuff," said Bruce. Not only doesn't he chop, but he doesn't use karate, either. His brand of beat-em-up is called Jeet Kune Do, one of the more specialized martial arts.

What's martial arts, one newsman wanted to know? That's ways to beat up people, Kato told him in so many words.

He may not do too much chopping, but he's always glad to break up an office for you, like he does in a new movie he's in, without his Kato mask. How about breaking somebody's neck, a newsman wanted to know? "Ah, now you are talking," said Bruce, "that's something more concrete!" This he can do. He also can blattey a 10-inch board with one good side kick.

Can a good dirty fighter beat up a good karate man? That depends on the man, says Bruce. "It's all in the attitude."

With the vast number of TV shows now in which women frequently bounce men off walls, the question of the day is can a woman really take a man who also knows how to fight? The newsman sighed with relief as Bruce assured them, "A woman can never whip a man."

Off the set, Bruce also runs martial arts studios and gives lessons himself—$500 for 10 lessons of 45 minutes each. "What do you learn after that?" "Oh, maybe how to give a good leg kick and then run like hell," Bruce laughed over his peach compote.

Two of his students right now are Hollywood tough guys Steve McQueen and James Coburn. "McQueen's got potential," Bruce said. "He's got the real killer's instinct."

Bruce looks at his skill an an art that is the expression of the self. "It's like a waltz," he says. Waltz right up to somebody and reduce them to a box of bones.

Bruce works out every day to keep in shape. A newsman wanted to know if he imbibed?

"Nope, don't drink or smoke," said Bruce. "No?" "No. But I do chew gum." "Chew gum? How come?" "Well, a lot of men smoke but Fu Manchu."

Miami Beach Sun, October 24, 1969

DON'T ORDER GUNG FU FROM BRUCE LEE

by Joe Maggio

You hear it all the time: "Yeah, man, I got a black belt. Karate. Yeah, you know, man." And then he gives you the hard stare while clenching and unclenching a fist or giving a side chopping movement with the side of his hand.

Of the thousands who practice the oriental art, and of the many hundreds who boast of having the coveted black belt, only a handful are in the good on the boast. To the ones of the "yeah, man, you know Karate's my bag" bit, I'd like to introduce Bruce Lee. The moment of truth. And if the boasters engage mano a mano with Lee, the moment of self-truth and possible injury.

The Chinese-born, Hong Kong-raised Lee is an office-wrecker par excellence as he demonstrates by demolishing James Garner's shabby office with his hands in his latest movie adventure, *Marlowe.*

"Gung Fu is a strictly Oriental skill," he says, while in Miami Beach to push the movie. "Unlike other forms of Karate, which promote static defense, Gung Fu and Jeet Kune Do are classically refined for self-defense and offensive aggression."

Lee, who played "Kato" on "The Green Hornet" series, has appeared in a number of TV shows including "Batman," "where I kicked the hell out of the Boy Wonder."

He doesn't have a black belt. He scoffs at those that make the claim. "There isn't time in a man's life, if he were to train the proper Oriental way, to receive such an honor. If Orientals can't earn it, surely Americans who practice one or two nights a week can't," he says while

Bruce Lee as the "office-wrecker par excellence" in a scene from the 1969 movie Marlowe, *starring James Garner (released by MGM Studios). Lee wrote on the back of this photograph that the light he smashed was "approximately eight feet" off the ground!*

engaging in a few thrusts and kicks with this writer.

"Of my art—Gung Fu and Jeet Kune Do—only one of ten thousand can handle it. It is martial art. Complete offensive attacks. It is silly to think almost anyone can learn it."

Bruce Lee has martial art studios in Seattle, Washington, and Oakland, where he trains a select few in his way of Karate.

"It isn't really contemporary forms of the art I teach. Mainly that which I work with—Martial Attack."

Lee sees a new vision in the movies. One of action, in which the combinations of all forms of defense and attack on the human body—Martial Art—will be the vanguard.

"There has been an era in movies that immortalized the western hero, the swordsman and now, if I can do it with James Coburn (*Our Man Flint*) in a new movie we both star in, *The Silent Flute*, Martial Art will be next."

The former University of Washington student ("where I was studying eastern philosophy until I was asked to play Kato in the Hornet series"), believes that this aggressive form of Karate shows an individual man's self-expression.

"It's really a smooth rhythmic expression of smashing the guy before he hits you, with any method available. Most Karate is defensive. You're taught to do something after it is done to you," the 29-year-old actor says.

Another film in which he demonstrated this carte blanche fighting was *The Wrecking Crew*, with Dean Martin.

While working on films and studying Christianity, Zen and Taoism, Lee participates in Karate tournaments throughout the world. He has won more than his share. A little shyly he says "about nine of ten I win."[9] This without a black belt.

Now, for the moment of truth. All you guys with those shiny black belts step forward. I thought so.

The Miami News Florida Report, October 24, 1969

CHOP TALK WITH AN ACTOR: MAYHEM UP HIS SLEEVE

by Ian Glass

Bruce Lee is inclined to curl his Oriental lip when you ask him about James Bond's karate exploits. Lee very decidedly knocks the technique of chopping someone on the side of the neck.

It is a laborious operation, he feels. Much better to jab one's pointed fingers into his face. After disabling him first by breaking his leg with a quick flip of the foot, of course. When Bruce whips that foot out, he brings the house down.

There is nothing bloodthirsty about the fellow, really, except perhaps for the demoralizing yells that accompany his lightening-quick [sic] movements. He just happens to be one of the world's foremost experts at the art of self-defense, and the creator of one form of it called Jeet Kune Do.

Lee, 28 years old, 145 pounds, 5-feet-7-inches tall, was in Miami briefly to tout the film *Marlowe*, which is coming here shortly. In this adaptation of a Raymond Chandler novel, Lee plays a villain who is hired to kill the hero, Philip Marlowe, played by James Garner.

"The name they gave me," said Lee, who has a bright, chirpy sense of humor, "was Winslow Wong. Well, OK, I'm Chinese. Grew up in Hong Kong. And 700 million Chinese can't be Wong."

Lee was discovered by the movies while demonstrating at the 1964 International Karate Tournament at Long Beach, Calif. "A producer said he wanted me to play a Chinese. I immediately could see the part—pigtails, chopsticks and 'ah-so's,' shuffling obediently behind the master who has saved my life. But it turned out to be better. I like acting very much. My next one—'The Silent Flute'—is going to be great. Has James Coburn in it. It will be full of the best self-defense artists in the world. We'll film it in Japan." Says he: "This was the year of the black man. The next year will be the year of the Oriental."

Between film-making, Lee teaches self-defense to film stars like Coburn and Steve McQueen—at $150 an hour or $500 for 10 hours. (He has 10 customers going hammer and tongs at the moment.) That's a lot to pay for learning how to beat up unfriendly strangers. But Jeet Kune Do is pretty special, according to Lee.

"Karate has become patternized, organized. I favor moving like a boxer; Jeet Kune Do offers more freedom, more self-expression. As for these people who chop boards in two…what a waste of time. I've yet to see a board hit back."

It's those high kicks, though, that make Lee lethal. His foot strikes like a cobra. Just watching it makes you sweat. It isn't his fault he falls from the 45th story of a building in the movie while in the act of demolishing hero Garner. It's obvious he landed on his feet, though.

The Star (Hong Kong) April 4, 1970

BRUCE QUITTING BOXING FOR ACTING

Famous Chinese boxer Bruce Lee, who teaches Steve McQueen and Roman Polanski the martial arts in Hollywood, made a surprise announcement in Hong Kong today—he plans to quit the boxing world.

"I am setting up a movie company with James Coburn and Stirling Silliphant," said the handsome boxing instructor who was once a Cantonese film star in Hong Kong.

Bruce talked to *The Star* in his Nathan Road home during his two-week Hong Kong holiday. He said he won't teach any Hong Kong students during his stay.

"Besides, I am too expensive. I charge US $150 an hour in United States," Bruce said.

"I'm tired of leading a life as a boxing instructor. It's time for me to start a business of my own. If my movie company is successful, it will bring me millions."

Bruce Lee was a Cantonese movie actor before he went to America ten years ago. In the United States he established himself as one of Hollywood's top boxing instructors as well as a TV actor. His quick rise to fame is the envy of Hollywood's dozens of karate and other boxing experts. Rumors have spread many times he had been killed.

"They all came from boxing instructors who are jealous of my success," Bruce believes.

James Coburn and Bruce Lee himself, will star in the first film Bruce's movie company is going to make, called *Silent Flute*. Shooting begins soon in India.

"We are hoping to get Roman Polanski as director, I have talked to him about this in Switzerland," Bruce told *The Star*.

The Washington Star ("Sportsweek" section), August 16, 1970

DON'T CALL IT KARATE—
IT'S MARTIAL ART

by J. D. Bethea

"You can't organize truth. That's like trying to put a pound of water into wrapping paper and shaping it," said actor and karate expert Bruce Lee, his dark eyes flashing.

Even for Lee, one of the best in the world, the search for perfection in the deadly art of Karate is a never-ending quest.[10]

When asked why they began studying karate, many of the guys who have risen to prominence in the field spout nice, little platitudes. Statements intended to show a purity of purpose. Not Lee. He says, simply, "I got tired of getting the hell beat out of me. I decided it was about time I learned how to whip hell out of the other guy."

That's how it began, in the streets of Hong Kong, the city in which the 20-year-old star was born.[11]

His father, a Chinese opera star, returned to the United States in 1959.[12] Lee smiles now when he thinks about some of those earlier days.

"Man. Do you know I worked for a newspaper back then?" he asked. "Yeah. I was an inserter at the Seattle Times. There I was folding those newspapers and things. Finally, I said the heck with this stuff. I'll teach martial arts."

Lee never refers to it as karate. For him it is always "the martial arts" and his "art form," which was evolved from the Wing Chun theory of karate that he studied in Hong Kong.[13] He calls his art form Jeet Kune Do. Jeet—meaning to stop or intercept. Kune—fist. Do—the ultimate reality.

During this period, reality for the slender, handsome Lee was living in Seattle and charging a big, fat $15 a month for lessons. His dream was to own karate schools all over the country.[14]

In 1964, however, three things happened to Lee that changed his direction. First, he got married. He and wife, Linda, now have two children. It was also in 1964 that he participated in a West Coast karate demonstration and met Jhoon Rhee. The two men immediately became friends. Rhee had begun his karate school the year before with only nine students.[15]

Through the years there has been a constant interchange between the young, somewhat irreverent Lee, who never had much patience with tradition, and Rhee, a 38-year-old master of the old school of Korean karate. The result, in addition to cementing their friendship, has been that each man has shifted slightly. Both have at times found it necessary to rethink their positions. Each has taken from the other that which will bring his own art form closer to truth.

Today, Rhee, owner of the ever-expanding Jhoon Rhee Institute of Tae Kwon Do, has branches dotting the Washington area. There are affiliates throughout the United States as well as a number of foreign countries. Rhee, a seventh-degree black belt, who has been referred to as the Pied Piper of Tae Kwon Do, is what Bruce Lee once wished to become.[16]

The final thing which changed Lee's direction was being discovered by Hollywood. Originally, he was going to be cast as Charlie Chan's "Number 1 Son" in a television series. It failed to materialize. But then came "The Green Hornet." Kids flocked to their television sets to watch Bruce Lee as Kato, putting his feet and fists through balsawood walls and doors and giving the bad guys hell.

The show folded after a while. This was a predictable outcome. Despite Lee's effectiveness and the adulation of the young set, "The Green Hornet" was an abysmally bad series. He began at $450 a week, was making $750 a week when the series ended and then asked himself, "What the hell do I do now?" Lee laughed out loud and leaned back on the sofa. He was in town on business and staying at Jhoon Rhee's Arlington home. They've come a long way since 1964.

Even though the Green Hornet and Kato were no more, Lee was not overly concerned about money at the time. As he often re-calls, "If money was what I wanted then, I'd have put up signs saying, 'Kato—Mothers, bring your little boys.'" Nevertheless, Lee did begin teaching again. He was primarily interested in teaching what he considered to be a "dedicated few." His fee? Twenty-six dollars an hour. He thought that was a substantial rate.

You can't organize truth. That's like trying to put a pound of water into wrapping paper and shaping it.

This changed, however, shortly after talking to one of TV producer William Dozier's assistants.[17] "He wanted to know what I was doing. I told the guy I was teaching again and he asked me what I was charging. Man, when I told him he said I was crazy. He said I should be charging $50 an hour. I thought about it and decided, why not $50 an hour?" That was when his "professional consultation and instruction" was cheap. Now $150 an hour might get you an appointment with Lee. Then again it might not.

Take movie director Roman Polanski, husband of slain actress Sharon Tate. He once had Lee fly to Gystadd [sic], Switzerland, for a short while just to receive private lessons.[18] Lee could have stayed on longer to instruct others for a couple of weeks at a nice, round $5,000 per week. But he declined. That's progress.

At first, it was easy to dismiss Lee's filmed expertise as the same old Hollywood stuff. Ironically, he's better than he was ever portrayed on celluloid. Three of his pupils, Joe Lewis, Chuck Norris and Mike Stone, have between them won every major karate tournament in the United States at least once. Lewis was Grand National champion three successive years. Lee handles and instructs these guys almost as a parent would a young child.[19] Which can be somewhat disconcerting to watch.

It's like walking into a saloon in the old west and seeing the fastest guy in the territory standing there with notches all over his gun. Then, in walks a pleasant little fellow who says, "How many times do I have to tell you you're doing it all wrong?" And the other guy listens. Intently.

Among his better-known Hollywood students, Lee also lists Steve McQueen, James Coburn, Stuart Whitman and writer Stirling Silliphant. Connections such as these can prove helpful. Lee, Coburn and Silliphant have entered into a joint venture for a movie called *Silent Flute*. Obviously, it is a martial arts film. Lee has plans for a series of such movies.

"It's about time we had an Oriental hero," he said. "Never mind some guy bouncing around the country in a pigtail or something. I have to be a real human being. No cook. No laundryman." Lee started whistling a theme from the movie and keeping beat on a coffee table. He looked like a happy kid. A very lethal, happy kid. But a happy kid just the same.

"In this movie there's something to appeal to different people on different levels. There's enough violence to satisfy almost anyone. Yet there's a study of man's evolution and attitude as Coburn meets people and finds death and love, looking for the ultimate truth." Lee hammers away at the importance of attitude in real life, too. "Suppose you come home and find some guys have battered a friend. First, you're going to think about *what* you should do. Then you're going to try to figure out *how*. But suppose, instead of a friend, you come home and find your mother battered. Wham! You're ready—that's pure attitude."

In Lee's philosophy there should be no method of fighting. There should only be tools to use as effectively as possible. "The highest art is no art. The best form is no form," Lee said, glancing at Jhoon Rhee with a smile. There are a number of points on which the two friends do not quite see eye-to-eye. For example, Lee is not interested in giving instruction to women. "There's just no way a woman is going to beat a man. Period," he says.

With the rising crime rate, however, karate schools like Jhoon Rhee's are flourishing throughout the country, and an increasingly large percentage of the students are women—the rationale apparently being that the average woman doesn't expect to get into a karate match with a man. She just wants a little bit of an edge when some guy grabs what he assumes is a defenseless woman.

"The trouble is that circumstances must dictate what you do," Lee continued. "But too many people are looking at 'what is' from a position of thinking 'what should be.'" Rhee nodded in approval. "Let me give you a good example why I don't like cults or sects in the martial arts," Lee said. "Let's take stances. Okay. Now look at the way a crane just stands there on one leg. So suppose you have something like that invented by a cripple? In 5,000 years everybody is a cripple."

They both laughed. Lee recalled his recent visit to Hong Kong and the glowing reception he received. "Everything was fine except the traffic. Los Angeles traffic is nothing. Some guy almost creamed me one day. Then he started giving me hell. I wanted to drag him out of that car and break him into pieces, but I knew I couldn't do that. Instead, I reached down and grabbed his nose and tried to twist it off. I felt a lot better."

That's Lee. Unorthodox, but effective. His method of dealing with future suitors for his daughter will probably work just as well. "It's simple," he said. "I'll just stand there after I tell him what time to have her back home. When he starts to leave I'll say 'wait a minute, I want you to look at something.'" Lee extended a fist. The knuckles were covered with large calluses, born of 13 years of breaking boards and bricks.[20]

"What do you want to bet the guy'll have her home early?"

Notes

1. © May 1967, *The Washington Post.* Reprinted by permission.

2. Lee returned to Hong Kong three months later—not three weeks.

3. The film executive was William Dozier, who "caught the act" indirectly through watching a 16mm film of Lee's demonstration.

4. Reprinted by permission of *The Seattle Times.*

5. Linda Lee Cadwell never took the name McCulloch. Her maiden name was Emery. Her father passed away when Linda was only five-years old and, years later, her mother remarried to a man named David McCulloch. However, Linda retained the name Emery.

6. Bruce Lee's second school was actually in Oakland—not San Francisco.

7. Meaning that Bruce Lee taught practitioners of these arts—Lee himself only taught his own art of Jeet Kune Do at this point in his life.

8. The answer actually is no. Lee was a top-notch gung fu expert, not a karate expert.

9. As Bruce Lee did not compete in karate tournaments this statement gives the false impression that he was a point-karate competitor, a practice for which he had no use.

10. Rather than seeking perfection "in the deadly art of karate," Bruce Lee sought to develop it within himself. His quest evolved from pure combat to a better understanding of the perpetually developing process of self-knowledge, using learning from interrelated aspects of martial art, philosophy, and humanity as a means of self-discovery.

11. Bruce Lee was actually thirty years old when he gave this interview.

12. Lee Hoi Chuen never returned to the United States after Bruce's birth in 1940. Bruce returned to the land of his birth in 1959.

13. Particularly in the final stages of its evolution, jeet kune do—Lee's own creation—was a completely separate art from Wing Chun. Although both possessed similarities, they also embodied substantial differences in methodology and educational emphasis. While both share a concern with combative efficiency, the methodologies employed by each of these arts are substantially different. It is also technically incorrect to refer to "the Wing Chun theory of karate," as karate is a Japanese art and Wing Chun is a form of the Chinese art of gung fu.

14. Bruce Lee's dream at this point in his life was not to own "karate schools all over the country," but rather gung fu institutions. In a letter written in September 1962 to an old family friend, Eva Tso, Bruce Lee said:

> My aim, therefore, is to establish a first Gung Fu Institute that will later spread out all over the U.S. (I have set a time limit of ten to fifteen years to complete the whole project.)...I may now own nothing but a little place down in a basement, but once my imagination has got up a full head of steam, I can see painted on a canvas of my mind a picture of a fine, big five- or six-story Gung Fu Institute with branches all over the States.

15. Jhoon Rhee's art was actually tae kwon do—a Korean, not a Japanese, martial art. However, tae kwon do is also known in the martial arts nomenclature as "Korean karate."

16. Bruce Lee never wished to become "The Pied Piper of Tae Kwon Do."

17. The assistant Bruce Lee spoke with was Charlie Fitzsimons, who recalled the following:

> During the shooting of the series, which only went thirteen episodes, he and I became very good friends. He was a young man. He was in his middle twenties and very enthusiastic about what he was doing. He had terrific personal ego, but he had no illusions about his lack of acting knowledge. He was quite humble about his ability to perform and yet had this amazing ego in real life. He had that unbeatable spirit. During the shooting of the series, and as we became friends, he would come to my house. I had young children at the time and we would have Chinese food together, which he would select and bring to my house. And he would come to me for advice and guidance from the older, as he thought, American. In truth, I was an immigrant—he was the American, having been born in this country. But he came to me, confidentially, on many areas in his life.
>
> When the series was cancelled, he was very concerned about whether or not he had a future in the industry, and that's where I say there was this strange combination of a humility as far as acting was concerned and yet this consuming power and ego that was in this young man. So he asked to have lunch with me....[We] met at Clifton's, as we often had, and it was to say how worried he was. He had a wife. He had a little baby. He lived in a small house in Culver City. He had not been paid a lot of money for "The Green Hornet," so there was no situation of having a savings account. And he wanted me to level with him as to whether I thought he had any future in the industry or whether he should just forget it.
>
> I told him at the time that I thought he had an exceptional personality—he had this exceptional magnetic energy—and that though there would never be a great demand for Oriental performers, I thought that, yes, he would have a career, and it was worth his while sticking with it.
>
> He then said to me "But how am I going to pay the bills in the meantime?"
>
> And I said how about using your great knowledge and adeptness in the martial arts? How about...teaching and using that to earn the necessary money you need for overhead?
>
> He said, "Well, I don't have the money to go out and rent a studio or to get equipment. It's not possible."
>
> I said "Wait a minute, Bruce. I have an idea. How about teaching people in their own homes, where you don't have to have a studio?"
>
> His next question was "Well where do I get clients and how do I do it?"
>
> So I said, "All right, then, I'm going to combine some Irish con with your Asian insight. I'm going to design a business card for you and some sta-

tionery. And I want you to go into business, a no-overhead business." And I designed, right at Clifton's Cafeteria, a business card which basically said on one side: "Bruce Lee, Master of the Martial Arts," or whatever it was— I've forgotten the exact words I used. And I put down "Professional consultation—$1,000." Then I turned the card over and on the other side I put "Private lessons, in the privacy of your own home." And I put down an outrageous figure, for a course of private lessons. [Editor's note: Bruce Lee simply used his own name and his own jeet kune do logo on his business cards. However, on some cards, he also put the rates that Charlie Fitzsimons suggested.] So I showed this to Bruce, and he looked at me and said, "You're out of your mind."

And I said "No I'm not." I explained to him that at that period in the sixties, the late-sixties in Hollywood, there was a middle-aged, macho syndrome. All of the middle-aged, would-be macho individuals in the motion picture industry and in business had all been caught up in this,…in having you know, their hair styled like the younger generation and wearing outrageously stupid clothes and so I said to Bruce "These are your potential clients. That's why I put down a thousand dollars for a 'professional consultation.'" And I said "The reason that the other price is outrageous is that that's the only thing that will impress them."

And he said, "But how do I, you know, how do I get to these people?"

I said to him, "You have a very good friend named Jay Sebring." Now Jay Sebring, in those days, was *the* hairdresser to the middle-aged machos. And it was very expensive in those days to have your hair styled. But he had access to all of them. They all went to Jay to have their hair styled. So I said to Bruce, "Why don't you have the card printed, give a large quantity of them to Jay at his studio, and ask Jay if he would be kind enough to give one to each of his hairdressing clients who qualify for that macho, middle-aged image? You'll get clients."

On the card, by the way, I had put down that there would be a telephone number. I had asked him to get a post office box in Beverly Hills—it had to be Beverly Hills. Jay Sebring did distribute the cards and Bruce did get the clients and in a very short period of time he was teaching martial arts to a lot of very wealthy, prominent gentlemen in the motion picture industry and allied industries.…He became so successful that he was able to move out of his humble home in Culver City that he had been worried about being able to pay the rent on, into a much more palatial home up on Mulholland Drive.

18. This is true. According to Bruce Lee's daytimer diaries, he taught Roman Polanski in Switzerland on February 20, 22, 23, 25, 26, and 27, 1970. In a letter to Linda, Lee reported: "One thing for sure, I got to know Roman a little bit more, and I feel this will help future development. [Lee had hoped to interest Polanski in directing his

screenplay for *The Silent Flute*.] If not, at least I have a friend, and a student. He has improved in his performance. I would like to be back on Tuesday, March 3rd and, believe me, Roman wants me to stay on and on."

19. This objective, third-party report on the nature of the teacher-student relationship between Bruce Lee and the three karate champions cited is refreshing in light of many of the unwarranted claims made after Lee's death by many of these same individuals that they had been Bruce Lee's "teacher." For example, according to Bruce Lee's daytimer diaries, Chuck Norris received personal instruction from Bruce Lee on October 20, November 17 and 24, and December 1, 1967; and January 5, 19, and 31, 1968. There is no evidence, however, of Bruce receiving any type of instruction from Chuck Norris.

20. The calluses on Bruce Lee's knuckles were more likely derived from hours spent punching the heavy bag and Makawara pad.

Part 4

THE
HONG KONG
YEARS

(1971–1973)

The Hong Kong Star, November, 1971

THE MAN WITH A STOMACH LIKE A BRICK WALL

by John Hardie

If you were to call Mr. Bruce Lee a punk—and for a self-confessed punk, why not?—he probably would turn the other cheek and smile. Admittedly, such a stringent insult applied to the average high-polished fool would enable the victim and his lawyer to retire happily on the proceeds.

But Bruce Lee, the first Oriental to make the Hollywood big time, can cop a fair amount of abuse.[1]* Yet touch this deceptively light man of 30 whose muscles ripple beneath a floral shirt and— POW! "I have a sure-fire temper, man," he said in an accent too un- mistakably American to be phoney. "I cannot bear anyone to touch me. Feel this," he said, a finger gesturing towards his taut midriff. Dismissing the preceding statement, I moved with trepidation and thumped. I could have been hitting a brick wall.

Bruce Lee smiled, dropped to the floor and began a series of push-ups—on one finger! "Someone once asked me," he said, "what I am going to do when I am 50 or 60. I replied, 'Man, there ain't going to be no 50 or 60-year-old that can push me around.'"

How did this meanest fighter around keep fit? "Every Monday, Wednesday and Friday, I work on my legs," he said. "Every Tuesday, Thursday and Saturday I work on my punch. On Wednesdays and Sundays, I have sparring sessions."

Rules

How did he fancy himself in the ring against Cassius Clay? Said Mr. Lee: "If you put on a glove, you are dealing in rules. You must know

---

*Notes for Part 4 begin on page 164.

the rules to survive. But in the street you have more tools in your favor—the kick, the throw, the punch."

For a man who has trained three world karate champions, and Steve McQueen and other Hollywood toughs, that, for my money, was good enough. To those who may not have known Mr. Lee until Hollywood exploited his talent, you may care to know he was born in San Fran-

A star is an illusion. Man, is that something that can screw you up. When the public calls you a star, you had better know that it's only a game.

cisco, came to Hong Kong when he was three months old and returned to the U.S. in 1959 where he majored in philosophy at the University of Washington.

He studied Chinese boxing during his years in Hong Kong and it was this learning he put into effect at the Long Beach International Karate Championships in 1964 that won him a break in Hollywood. Spotted by 20th Century [Fox], he was cast in the television series "The Green Hornet," an ultimate failure, he admits, which ran only one season. But more roles followed. There were chances in "Ironside," "Batman" and the widely acclaimed "Longstreet," starring James Franciscus. Now he finds himself a juicy ham in the middle of a sandwhich as contract.

Back in Hong Kong to complete a film for Golden Harvest, he said: "I have seen a script for a TV series on Chinese martial art called 'The Warrior.'[2] This is the thing I really want to do." I said the contract should be something of a financial bonanza but here was a man equally as objective with words as muscles.

"My policy is that money is an indirect matter," he said. "The direct matter is your ability or what you are going to do that counts. If that comes, the indirect things will follow. What I am trying to do is start a whole trend of martial art films in the U.S. To me, they are much more interesting than the gun-slinging sagas of the West. In the Westerns you are dealing solely with guns. Here we deal with everything. It is an expression of the human body."

What then did he think of the blood-thirsty Chinese movies? "You have to be careful," said Mr. Lee, "of movies that have broadly an action kick. It does not matter, it seems, whether a Chinese movie has a central theme as long as there are so many feet of action. I don't go for that and I have achieved mutual cooperation with Golden Harvest in the sense that we are going 50/50—still with the main theme in mind."

What opportunities did he see for other Asian movie stars in Hollywood? "None for the next 10 years," he said, and followed with a whirlwind attack on the "stars." "A star is an illusion. Man, is that something that can screw you up. When the public calls you a star, you had better know that it's only a game. Since 1969, I have been really willing this TV series to happen. At that time, I wanted all the indirect things—money, fame, the big opening nights. Now I have it, or am beginning to get it, the whole thing doesn't seem important any more. I have found that doing a thing is more important. I am having fun doing it."

Bruce Lee shook my hand. It crunched in his grip but it was good to meet a man with brains to match his brawn.

The Star (Hong Kong), November 4, 1971

BRUCE LEE'S $1 MILLION PUNCH

Chinese boxing expert Bruce Lee has delivered a tremendous punch at the box office—his new film has raked in $1 million in just three days. This figure is a record and has stunned the local movie world.

The action packed movie, *The Big Boss*, hit the magical million dollar mark after opening at 16 theaters.[3] Takings were

Bruce Lee in The Big Boss *(released in North America as* Fists of Fury)*, the movie that smashed box office records throughout Southeast Asia and set Bruce Lee on his way to becoming the world's first Asian superstar.*

$372,000 for the first day alone. This fantastic record must make other studio bosses wonder if local audiences have had their fill of swordplay movies.

There is no doubt that Bruce Lee, the man with the iron stomach, is the secret of the film's success.

Skill

He shows his great skill at Chinese boxing in many scenes. And it is he who wins most applause from the audience. The film tells of the struggle of overseas Chinese in Bangkok who live in fear of gangsters. Popular young actress Yee Yee is the female lead and turns in a good performance. Lo Wei directed the movie, adding to his already impressive list of achievements. The film is showing at three major theater chains—Queen's, Hoover and Lee.

The producers of the film could hardly have forseen it would be such a big hit. But Bruce Lee is well known in Hong Kong and with the martial arts popular here, the formula proved a winner.

Sunday Post-Herald (Hong Kong), November 21, 1971

BRUCE LEE—THE $3 MILLION BOX-OFFICE DRAW

The new superstar of Mandarin films

by Jack Moore

The first thing Bruce Lee does when he meets somebody is to give them the most athletic handshake this side of the International Date Line. The recipient of the handshake generally spends the following half-hour or so sitting around and gingerly counting his knuckles, just to make sure they are all still there.

Lee, in case you have been hiding in a cave for the last few months, is the newest superstar in the Mandarin film world, and he reached the position chiefly by being a very tough guy indeed, trained in bare-handed combat and stuff like that.

It wasn't until after he made his first film *The Big Boss*, in fact, that most people discovered he was a heck of a good actor as well as being a formidable fistfighter. In an interview this week, Bruce said he'd rather act than fight anyway. "When I decided to come back to Hong Kong and do the film for Raymond Chow, I prepared by going to see a whole bunch of Mandarin movies," he said. "They were awful. For one thing, everybody fights all the time, and what really bothered me was that they all fought exactly the same way. Wow, nobody's really like that. When you get into a fight, everybody reacts differently, and it is possible to act and fight at the same time."

He says he tried to do just that in *The Big Boss,* and it obviously worked. At the time of the interview, the box-office receipts for the film were well above $3 million and climbing.

"We knew from the outset that the film was going to be a success, but I have to admit we weren't really expecting it to be that successful." (For the benefit of those cave-hiders mentioned earlier, *The Big Boss* early this month broke the record set several years ago by *The Sound of Music,* to become the most financially successful motion picture to ever play in Hong Kong.)

"What I hope is that the movie will represent a new trend in Mandarin cinema. I mean, people like films that are more than just one long armed hassle. With any luck, I hope to make multi-level films here—the kind of movies where you can just watch the surface story if

Everything is overplayed in Mandarin films. To make really good ones, you'd have to use subtlety, and very few people in the business want to risk any money by trying that.

you want, or you can look deeper into it if you feel like it. Most of the Chinese films to date have been very superficial and one dimensional. I tried to do that in *The Big Boss.* The character I played was a very simple, straightforward guy. Like, if you told this guy something, he'd believe you. Then, when he finally figures out he's been had, he goes animal. This isn't a bad character, but I don't want to play him all the time. I'd prefer somebody with a little more depth."

Bruce's first screen appearance here was about two and a half years ago in a flick called *Marlowe,* a detective film starring James Garner. Bruce played a thug named Winslow Wong. Nobody seemed to notice at the time, but now the film has been brought back.

"They're giving me top billing, too," said Lee. "I really don't know how to explain that to Garner when I get back to Hollywood." Garner, along with an astounding number of other people, has studied Chinese boxing under Bruce's direction.[4]

In fact, that's how Lee got into the entertainment business in the first place. "After I left the University of Washington in Seattle where I was studying—are you ready for this?—philosophy, I planned to open a whole bunch of schools, teaching martial arts. I started off in basements and parking lots and places like that, and then eventually I started teaching actors. I used to make very good bread doing that, man. I started charging US $500 for a 10-hour course, and wound up doubling it. Steve McQueen was one of my students. So was James Coburn. Just about the time I discovered that I really didn't want to teach self-defense for the rest of my life, I went to the Long Beach International Karate Tournament and got myself discovered by Hollywood. That was 1964. Naturally, I was signed up to play the Number One Son of Charlie Chan, only the movie never got made. Then I got into the 'Batman' series, and finally did a season playing Kato in 'The Green Hornet.' You know why I got that Green Hornet job? I'll tell you why I got that Green Hornet job. Because the hero's name was Britt Reid, and I was the only Chinese in all of California who could pronounce Britt Reid, that's why. Anyway, it was fun, and after that, I did this really beautiful television thing for a series called 'Longstreet.' James Franciscus played a blind dude who was out for revenge, and I played a guy who was getting him ready for a fight."

(At this point in the interview, this really wild, far-away look came over his face and he started quoting dialogue from the script. The thing was written by Stirling Silliphant, who is THE great screen writer of all time). "The thing was called 'The Way of the Intercepting Fist,'[5] and the lines went 'Listen, man, can you hear the wind, and can you hear the birds singing? You have to HEAR it.

Empty your mind, man. You know how water fills a cup? It BECOMES that cup. You have to be ready, man. You have to think about nothing. You have to BECOME nothing.'"

Really gorgeous dialogue, it was, and Bruce obviously loved doing the scene. Everybody else loved it too, including America's usually unimpressionable television critics. *The New York Times* did a review and suggested that Bruce was so good he should have a TV series of his own. Which is what's happening now.

"I should find out within a week whether this thing is on. If so, I will hustle back to Hollywood to make a pilot for a series called "The Warrior," which is a really freaky adventure series. It's about a Chinese guy who has to leave China because he managed to kill the wrong person, and winds up in the American West in 1860. Can you dig that? All these cowboys on horses with guns and me with a long, green hunk of bamboo, right? Far out."

Bruce comes pretty close to being the ultimate Mid-Pacific Man, what with all sorts of good things happening, career-wise, on both sides of the ocean. Right now, he's making a second film for Golden Harvest which could prove as big a winner as *The Big Boss,* worrying about the proposed Hollywood TV series and planning about six other things.

His background and training has been acquired in both the Far East and the Far West, and he has even managed to have a couple of really international children, one of whom he describes as "a six-and-a-half year-old brown-haired, blue-eyed Chinese kid. He's a gas."

Bruce's father had an outstanding career in Chinese opera, an art form that really interests Bruce. "It's one-dimensional, but it's really stylized and formal, and very groovy indeed. But it's not my bag. What I'm doing now is trying to find out exactly what is my bag, and I think 'The Warrior' series might help me discover. What's holding things up now is that a lot of people are sitting around in Hollywood trying to decide if the American television audience is ready for an Oriental hero.[6] We could get some really peculiar reactions from places like the Deep South. I was a little worried because a series like this means all kinds of work, like 365 days a year. But finally I said 'I'm gonna do the series one way or the other—damn the torpedoes, full speed ahead and so forth,' and I decided to plunge right in."

Aside from the hang-up of whether the United States thinks Bruce is too exotic to be a TV hero, he also has the additional worry of Far Eastern audiences thinking he's too Western. "There were some scenes in *The Big Boss* where I really didn't think I was Chinese enough," he said. "You really have to do a lot of adjusting."

Empty your mind, man. You know how water fills a cup? It BECOMES that cup. You have to be ready, man. You have to think about nothing. You have to BECOME nothing.

Not that Bruce is suffering from any kind of identity crisis, as any Mid-Pacific Man might be expected to do. He's so busy at the moment he hasn't had time to develop anything like that. He even worries about arcane things like artistic progress of the Mandarin cinema (which, he says, will only be possible when local directors get off their individual ego trips and studios start paying better money for better quality).[7]

As for his own contributions to the betterment of Mandarin movies, he thinks maybe he can keep it up by simply not making any films that he personally does not consider quality material. "Everything is overplayed in Mandarin films. To make really good ones, you'd have to use subtlety, and very few people in the business want to risk money by trying that. On top of which, the scripts are pretty terrible. You wouldn't believe all the stuff I re-wrote for *The Big Boss*. Still, with a lot of work and some luck, there's no reason why the quality of Mandarin movies can't be improved all round. Quality has to come first. Bruce Lee, Raymond Chow, all of us have to be secondary to the quality of the film itself."[8]

Which has to be the most encouraging thing the Mandarin film world has heard in a long, long time.

THE BIG BOSS TAKES A RECORD PROFIT

The Big Boss grossed a total of $3.2 million during its local run which ended yesterday. About 1.2 million film goers have paid to see this Golden Harvest production starring Bruce Lee. The film, having bossed the local screens for 19 days, outgrossed the last record-holder, *The Sound of Music*, by about $800,000.

The Julie Andrews film has been local film distributors' wildest dream at the box-office since it hit the screens in 1966. It is generally believed among local film businessmen that *The Big Boss* has done so well that its record is unlikely to be equalled by any film in the future.

Meanwhile, Bruce Lee has returned from filming *The Intercepting Fists* in Macao this week.[9] He bluntly turned down the fight

Bruce Lee taking five on the set of The Big Boss *with his co-star Han Ying Chieh (who played Mi, "The Boss"). Although Han Ying Chieh is credited as "fight arranger" for* The Big Boss, *it is well known that Lee did most of his own fight choreography for the film.*

challenge by yet another Hong Kong boxer, Chan Shing-biu. The challenges have been arriving daily since the film was shown. Chan, 59, challenged Bruce to tackle a candidate chosen among his students. "I find this sort of thing really annoying," Bruce said. "I am not going to fight with anybody," he added.

The China Mail (Hong Kong), November 22, 1971

MIDAS BRUCE TO MAKE NEW FILM

by H. S. Chow

Bruce Lee has the Midas touch. It's almost certain that his second film, *The Intercepting Fists*, will again make millions. This is veteran film distributor, Mr. S. T. Wu's opinion. He said this after studying the box-office results of *The Big Boss*, which grossed a record $3.2 million in 19 days.

The Big Boss broke two other records:

- It was the first film to become a million-dollar grosser after the second day of its local run.
- It was the only film that could attract a full house seven shows a day.

Mr. Wu said the film was still going strong at some better-located theaters on its final day last week. "Putting all these together, I reckon Bruce's second film will gross no less than $2 million," he said. He said that Bruce's boxing skill was the main point in his favor as a top attraction. "People like him. They leave the theaters with the intention of seeing more of the star in the future."

Mr. Wu stressed that few stars have such an effect on the public. He predicted that *The Big Boss* will no doubt make other Mandarin films change their image—switching from swordplay to hand-to-hand combat. And things would have to be done in a believable level—people are simply becoming fed up with superpower feats that are physically impossible to achieve. He said the new trend will benefit our film industry in the long run.

BRUCE'S OPINION ON KUNG FU, MOVIES, LOVE AND LIFE

by Hsin Hsin

Chatting with Bruce Lee, I have a very deep impression—through the use of different methods, he can control his emotions. This is the basic quality of a good actor.

After *The Big Boss* was shown, Bruce Lee immediately became a very popular figure. Everybody is talking about him and his film. How can *The Big Boss* have such a good record? How did Bruce become so extraordinary? But most people do not want to find the reason, they simply praise this great teacher of Kung Fu.

Because he has become the "star of stars" in just two or three months, everybody wants to know more about his real self—his attitude towards life and so on.

Through the help of Golden Harvest Company, I had a chance to meet Bruce in the studio in Ngau Chi Wan. This is the second time I have met him. The first time we met was in the cinema—I saw him on the screen.

After a short conversation, I felt that Bruce was the same Bruce I saw on the screen. He is muscular. He moves as he likes. The only difference between

Although perhaps best known for his pioneering work in the martial arts and in elevating the level of the martial arts film genre, Bruce Lee was also a profound thinker and philosopher who loved to discuss issues such as human relationships, the nature of man, and how to live a productive and fulfilling life.

"Cheng Chiu-on" on the screen and Bruce is that the real Bruce is warmer and more emotional.[10] With his rich and low voice, he is indeed a man of strength.

His voice is rich and fast. His attitude is sincere. He can easily impress you. However, if you are not careful, you may miss some of his nuggets of wisdom. If you are careful, his clear sentences will remain in your memory forever.

The most valuable point is that although he has stayed in the U.S. for many years, his knowledge of Chinese is still sufficient. He can use words properly. This shows that his cultivation in these two languages is very deep.

That day, Bruce's conversation was very spectacular and systematic, so I have used the dialogue form to report it:

One Cannot Be Too Traditional and Narrow

Question: What is your opinion on the relation between a husband and wife?

Bruce Lee: I think when a couple marry, they either go into heaven or live in hell. They may live a fairly like life [sic], or they may suffer a lot. I am a fortunate man. I am fortunate not because my film can break a record, but because I have a good wife, Linda. She is unsurpassed. Why do I say this? First, I believe, a couple should develop a kind of friendship. It can also happen among our friends. Linda and I have this kind of friendship. We understand each other, like a pair of good friends. We thus can stay happily together. The quality in Linda that moves me is her neutral love for me. She treats our relationship with calmness, objectivity and neutrality. I think this is the kind of attitude that a couple should adopt. For example, if I state a point, my wife has her idea. Certainly we ought to discuss things or it would be difficult for us to get along well. The happiness we have today is built on the ordinary life we had before we married. The happiness that is got from ordinary life can last longer: like coal, it burns gradually and slowly. The happiness that is got from excitement is like a brilliant fire—soon it will go out. Before we married, we never had the chance to go to nightclubs. We only spent our nights watching TV and chatting. Many young couples live a very exciting life when they are in love. So, when they marry, and their lives are reduced to calmness and dullness, they will feel impatient and will drink the bitter cup of a sad marriage.

Question: Do you think that an inter-racial marriage will face unsolvable obstacles?

Bruce Lee: Many people may think that it will be [sic]. But to me, this kind of racial barrier does not exist. If I say I believe that "everyone under the sun" is a member of a universal family, you may think that I am bluffing and idealistic. But if anyone still believes in racial differences, I think he is too backward and narrow. Perhaps he still does not understand man's equality and love. Many people are still bound by tradition. When the elder generation says no to something, they strongly disapprove of it. If they say that something is wrong, they also believe that it is wrong. They seldom use their mind to find out the truth and seldom express sincerely their real feeling. In fact, tradition is nothing but a formula laid down by experience. As we progress and time changes, it is necessary to reform this formula. For example, some people fight against each other because they believe in different religions. Actually, if they think a bit more, they will not fight for such a foolish cause. Similarly, box-office success is a formula, but will I forget my food and sleep for this dead formula? I, Bruce Lee, am a man who never follows those fearful formulas. So, no matter if your color is black or white, red or blue, I can still make friends with you without any barrier. Here, I can frankly say, I am glad that you are here, for I know that you do not aim to simply take a few photographs and make some money from it.

Without a Sufficient Reason, He Never Fights

Question: Thank you. Now I want to ask a difficult question. In Hong Kong, the number of murders is increasing annually. Many people believe it is the end result of the so-called "Kung Fu movie." If you make a movie that has a bad influence on people, will you feel sorry for it?

Bruce Lee: Good question. However, before I answer this question, I have to make one point clear. That is, a movie is not made by Bruce Lee alone and one can never dictate the quality of a film. It is the product produced first by the script-writer, then the director, actors and a lot of working members. So, if I really make a movie that has a bad influence on its audience, I should not bear the whole responsibility. Nevertheless, I still have the following wishes: One, I never want to make a movie for the sake of cruelty. I will first examine the reasons why the characters have to fight. Are these reasons sufficient?

Through the ages, the end of heroes is the same as ordinary men. They all died and gradually faded away in the memory of man. But when we are still alive, we have to understand ourselves, discover ourselves and express ourselves.

If not, I will not join in. Two, because martial art is my career, I want to use it as a means to express my ideals. A real fighter should fight for righteousness. Moreover, when he decides to fight, he must be sincere and fight wholeheatedly to the end. Only in such a way can he develop good character and total truth and sincerity. Like the way I am talking now, I am being totally sincere and am prepared to tell you all that I know. And I am trying my best to answer your questions. If everyone does a thing wholeheartedly and sincerely for their ideals, then money will become a secondary question. However, I can see that in film-making, not many people have principles to follow. Most are speculators, they do everything for money. They propagandize violence and cruelty for no reason in films.

The Most Important Thing Is Self-Realization

Question: The box-office record of *The Big Boss* proves that you are a very successful movie star. Do you want to climb higher? And have you prepared for the day when you will fall from the ladder of success? *Bruce Lee:* As I have said before, success means doing something sincerely and whole-heartedly. And you have to have the help of other people to achieve it. As for the idea of getting higher, I think that it is very absurd, it is only a fantasy. It cannot be obtained just by sitting there and wishing. I think life is a process. Through the ages, the end of heroes is the same as ordinary men. They all died and gradually faded away in the memory of man. But when we are still alive, we have to understand ourselves, discover ourselves and express ourselves. In this way, we can progress, but we may not be successful. I have said before, "truth" is nowhere to be found on a map. Your truth is different from that of mine. At first, you may think that this is truth, but later you discover another truth and then the former truth is denied. But, you are closer to truth. So, although today I am successful, I will still continue to discover myself. But whether I can "climb higher" is still a fantasy. A man is at his worst when he does not understand himself, this is especially true of people in the film industry. Stars rise and then fall. This is not surprising. Many of them do not understand themselves, so after their failure, they will feel disheartened. They should ask themselves if they had any substantial reason to support their success, or if they succeeded through luck. If they are willing to calm down and re-examine themselves, they will feel better. But, I find that many stars are not like this. When they succeed, they are blind, thinking that they are the greatest star in the world. So, in the end, when the god of luck leaves them, they feel unfortunate.

A Good Wife Is the Greatest Happiness

Question: You now have a lot of things to do. You certainly don't have much chance to stay at home. Does your wife ever complain?
Bruce Lee: I have thought this over too. I now have tried to find time to stay with my family. I always ask myself: "Does my work affect her mood?" When I find that it does, I will reject some of the contracts. But Linda is really excellent, she never complains. She understands me, she knows that I must struggle and it is worth any

sacrifice. I thank her very much for this. At the same time, I also practice Gung Fu, very often I use her to exude my energy. Yet she still accepts it joyously. With such a good wife, how can I ask for more?

The China Mail (Hong Kong), July 25, 1972

ACTION MAN BRUCE LIKES THE QUIET LIFE...

by H. S. Chow

Life as Hong Kong's most sought-after actor is too complicated for Bruce Lee. Having led a simple, quiet life in the United States for so long, he finds it hard to cope with things here.

"I don't feel like social gatherings," he said. "Nor am I interested in publicizing myself. But such things are simply unavoidable in a star's life. Particularly in a small place like Hong Kong."

To make it worse, he said, he often finds himself being confronted by people who try to be nice to him. But he doubts whether they do it for friendship or for their own gain.

Expectations

Bruce regrets that he's misunderstood by film bosses. "They think I am only interested in money," he said. "That's why they all try to lure me onto their set by promising me huge sums and nothing else. But, at heart, I only want a fair share of their profit. What I long for is to make a real good movie. But, unfortunately, few local producers can live up to my expectations. In fact, I would be quite happy to sit down for a long talk with any one who takes filming seriously. I would be quite satisfied even if it's just talks."

Bruce has so far worked only in three Mandarin films, all with

Golden Harvest. Although many lucrative offers have been made to him, he doesn't know exactly what his next film will be like or who's going to make it.

"It can be produced by Shaws, Golden Harvest, or any film company," he continued. "It has never been my intention to be tied to a particular company."

Bruce enjoys spending his leisure at home, with his American wife, Linda, and their two children, aged three and seven. A married couple, who has been living with them for many years, help run the household.[11] Bruce said his family life would seem quite banal to most people. But he stressed that it's through banality that he enjoys life.

"I would be quite happy to sit down for a long talk with anyone who takes filming seriously." Bruce Lee finds an opportunity for such a discussion on the set of The Big Boss.

Bruce does regular running exercises. He has been in the habit of taking a two-mile run up and down the Waterloo Hill Road area every day around 4 PM. It takes him about 14 minutes. A martial arts exponent, he used to spend hours a day for six days a week training in punch and kick.

"I did it this way," he said, "I trained my hands every Monday, Wednesday and Friday—and my legs on the alternate days." Bruce said such exercise came to a halt when he came to Hong Kong, but it will be resumed very soon when the equipment is shipped here from his U.S. home.

Bruce, 31, married Linda eight years ago when they were studying at the University of Washington. Bruce majored in philosophy and his wife was a medical student.

ME AND JEET KUNE DO

by Bruce Lee

When I returned from Thailand with the work crew of Golden Harvest Ltd. after the completion of *The Big Boss*, many people started asking me this: What was it that made me give up my career in the States and return to Hong Kong to shoot Chinese films?

Perhaps the general feeling was that it was all hell to have to work on Chinese films since the Chinese film industry was still so underdeveloped. To the above question, I find no easy explanation except that I am Chinese and I have to fulfill my duty as a Chinese.

The truth is, I am an American-born Chinese. My identity as a Chinese is beyond all doubts. At least I have always looked upon myself as a Chinese during all my years in the States, and in the eyes of the Westerners I am of course a Chinese.

Being a Chinese, I must possess the basic requisites. By these requisites, I refer to the truthful representation of the culture and the display of the emotions of being a Chinese.

That I should become an American-born Chinese was accidental, or it might have been my father's arrangement. At that time, the Chinese inhabitants in the States, mostly migrated from the province of Kwangtung, were very much homesick. Nostalgia was held towards everything that was associated with their homeland. In this context, Chinese opera, with its unmistakably unique Chinese characteristics, won the day. My old man was a famous artist of the Chinese opera and was popularly accepted by the people. Hence he spent a lot of time performing in the States. I was born when he brought along my mother during one of his performance trips.

Yet, my father did not want me to receive an American education. When I reached three months of age, he sent me back to

Hong Kong—his second homeland—to live with his kinsmen. It could have been a matter of heredity or environment, I came to be greatly interested in the making of films when I was studying in Hong Kong. My father was then well-acquainted with lots of movie stars and directors, among whom there was the late Mr. Chin Kam. They brought me into the studio and gave me some roles to play. I started off as a bit player and gradually became the star of the show.

Even in discussion, Bruce Lee was quick to demonstrate his views on martial art. During an appearance on Hong Kong TVB's "Enjoy Yourself Tonight," he showed host Joseph Lau an element of his kicking philosophy.

That was a very crucial experience in my life. For the first time I was confronted with genuine Chinese culture. The sense of being part of it was so strongly felt that I was enchanted. I didn't realize it then, nor did I see how great an influence environment had on the molding of one's character and personality. Nevertheless, the notion of "being Chinese" was then duly conceived.

A Pugnacious Childhood

From boyhood to adolescence, I presented myself as a troublemaker and was greatly disapproved of by my elders. I was extremely mischievous, aggressive, hot-tempered and fierce. Not only my "opponents" of more or less my age stayed out of my way, but even the adults sometimes gave in to my temper. I never knew what it was that made me so pugnacious. The first thought that came into my mind whenever I met somebody I disliked was: "Challenge him!" Challenge him with what? The only concrete thing that I could think of were my fists. I thought that victory meant beating down others, but I failed to realize that victory gained by way of force was not real victory. When I enrolled in the University of Washington and was enlightened by philosophy, I regretted all my previous immature assumptions.

Why Did I Study Philosophy?

My majoring in philosophy was closely related to the pugnacity of my childhood. I often ask myself these questions: What comes after victory? Why do people value victory so much? What is "glory"? What kind of "victory" is "glorious"? When my tutor assisted me in choosing my courses, he advised me to take up philosophy because of my inquisitiveness. He said, "philosophy will tell you what man lives for."

When I told my friends and relatives that I had picked up philosophy, they were all amazed. Everybody thought I had better go into physical education since the only extra-curricular activity that I was interested in, from my childhood until I graduated from my secondary school, was Chinese martial arts. As a matter of fact, martial arts and philosophy seem to be antithetical to each other. But I think that the theoretical part of Chinese martial arts seems to be getting indistinct. Every action should have its why and wherefore; and there ought to be a complete and proficient theory to back up the whole concept of Chinese martial arts. I wish to infuse the spirit of philosophy into martial arts, therefore I insist on studying philosophy.

I have never discontinued studying and practicing martial arts. While I am tracing the source and history of Chinese martial arts, this doubt always comes up: Now that every branch of Chinese Gung Fu has its own form, its own established style, are these the original intentions of their founders? I don't think so. Formality could be a hindrance to progress; this is applicable to everything, including philosophy. The founder of any branch of Chinese Gung Fu must be more ingenious than the common man. If his achievement is not carried on by disciples of the same ingenuity, then things will only become formalized and get stuck in a cul-de-sac; whereby breakthrough and progress will be almost impossible.

Words of the Dragon

Neither Formality nor Branches

It is this understanding that makes me forsake all that I have learned before about forms and formality. Actually, I never wanted to give a name to the kind of Chinese Gung Fu that I have invented, but for convenience sake, I still call it "Jeet Kune Do." However, I want to emphasize that there is no clear line of distinction between "Jeet Kune Do" and any other kind of Gung Fu for I strongly object to formality, and to the idea of distinction of branches. What is Jeet Kune Do? Chinese martial art, definitely! It is a kind of Chinese martial art that does away with the distinction of branches, an art that rejects formality, and an art that is liberated from tradition.

Use Your Brain to Overcome Your Enemy

The two most important aspects of martial art are the "essence" and the "practicality." Essence refers to the foundation. It is only on a sound base that practical usage of Gung Fu could be realized. Swiftness, strength and persistence are the keywords to martial art. Jeet Kune Do rejects all restrictions imposed by forms and formality and emphasizes the clever use of mind and body to defend and attack.

It is ridiculous to attempt to pin down so-and-so's type of Gung Fu as "Bruce Lee's Jeet Kune Do." I call it Jeet Kune Do just because I want to emphasize the notion of deciding at the right moment in order to stop the enemy at the gate. If people are determined to call my actions "Do," this action can be called Jeet Kune Do.[12] In *Fist of Fury*, I had a fight scene with Robert Baker, who played the Russian boxer in the film. You may recall in this scene that he locked my neck with his legs so that I became unable to move. The only movable part of my body was my mouth—so I gave him a bite!

I am not joking. Really there is no rigid form in Jeet Kune Do. All that there is is this understanding: If the enemy is cool, stay cooler than him; if the enemy moves, move faster than him; be concerned with the ends, not the means; master your own manipulation of force, don't be restricted by your form.

Many friends of mine do show their concern for my past, let bygones be bygones! I have defeated some champions of the international martial arts competitions in America and for that have been proclaimed a "heavyweight" in the field of martial arts—but that was mean-

Every action should have its why and wherefore; and there ought to be a complete and proficient theory to back up the whole concept of Chinese martial arts. I wish to infuse the spirit of philosophy into martial arts, therefore I insist on studying philosophy.

ingless. That was only a show of brute courage and a fortuitous victory. As I have said, I changed my viewpoint after I had got in touch with philosophy. There is a Chinese saying: "Don't be conceited." Every Gung Fu teacher cites this to their students as a reminder.

A New Realm in Martial Arts

Philosophy brings my Jeet Kune Do into a new realm in the sphere of martial arts, and Jeet Kune Do brings my acting career to a new horizon. The filming experience of my childhood years was pastime only. Later, the producers in Hollywood, thinking that my martial art could be an attraction, invited me to play a role in their films. The television series "The Green Hornet" is an example. At this moment, I found that it was meaningless to go on shooting movies like that because I did not fit in with my roles. This is not to say that I could not play my roles well. The truth is: I am a yellow-faced Chinese, I cannot possibly become an idol for Caucasians, not to mention rousing the emotions of my countrymen. Because of this, I decided to come back to serve the Chinese film industry.

It was of course a sense of yearning for my homeland that drove me back to Hong Kong.[13] My friends were all telling me that I would earn much less in Hong Kong than in the States. But money is not all that important to me. The savings I made during the last few years should enable me to lead a fairly comfortable life. I am of the opinion that if the main objective of living is earning money, then we will gradually become the slave of money and all individuality and personality will be lost. Nevertheless, I do agree that it would be nice to be able to earn more under a clear conscience.

One thing that upset me very much before deciding to come back to shoot Chinese films was that somebody wrote me a letter, telling me that he "had agreed" to my coming back. He offered me 10,000 Hong Kong dollars. As for the choice of director or the content of the script, I was told not to bother.

Was This What I Wanted

Afterwards, a contract was made between a representative of Golden Harvest Ltd. and me. Mr. Raymond Chow appeared to me a man of insight and his Golden Harvest Ltd. a promising enterprise. They were, as a company, utilizing practical and efficient methods to promote towards the ideal of a better film industry: like encouraging independent productions, giving freedom to directors and actors to explore and manifest their talents. Therefore, I agreed to act in two films, the one being *The Big Boss* and the other being *Fist of Fury.*

At first I never expected that these two films could arouse such enthusiasm from the public. I wasn't bent on making a record when the shooting went under way. I just did my best. It came as a surprise that *The Big Boss* made a booking record of 3,180,000 Hong Kong dollars.

Therefore I finally decided to close down all my business in America and put my full heart in filming. And now, Mr. Raymond Chow and I have formed the Concord Production Company. Under the full support of Golden Harvest Ltd., we are starting to film *The Way of the Dragon.*

I dare not say that I am coming up to any achievement, but

this is the beginning of my career in Chinese movies. *The Big Boss* and *Fist of Fury* are the bridge leading me to paying full devotion to the Chinese film industry. On this bridge, I find the truth: A Chinese is, and always will be, a Chinese; I am a Chinese, I had better shoot Chinese films![14]

New Nation (Singapore), August 14, 15, and 16, 1972[15]

INSIDE BRUCE LEE

by Pang Cheng Lian

I. Watching the big boss at work

August is an impossible month to work in Hong Kong. The heat is unbearable—daily temperature is 33 degrees C (91 degrees F)—and the humidity, which is well over 70 percent, makes life uncomfortable and unpleasant.

This morning is typical of Hong Kong's oppressive and sultry summer. By the time I arrive at the Golden Harvest film studios, my handkerchief is wet with my perspiration. (It is definitely not in anticipation of talking to the latest superstar in the Chinese film industry—Bruce Lee Hsiao Loong.)[16]

Big stars, I have been warned, make it a point never to be punctual. So although Bruce Lee, who has turned director for his third Golden Harvest film, *The Way of the Dragon*, is scheduled to start work at 9 AM, I prepare to sweat it out for another half-an-hour before meeting the Big Boss.

The time by my watch is only 9:30 AM. But this box-office breaker is apparently atypical of his predecessors. For lying stationary in the studio's parking lot is his jazzy-looking scarlet convertible Mercedes Benz 350 SL—worth a cool $41,000.[17] The owner, I am told, has been here since 9 AM and was now in the studio watching a different director shooting another historical drama.

Naturally I head for the lot immediately. But I find it in semi-darkness and it is difficult to make out which of the numerous men is the million-dollar actor I met last March. He spots me, however, and I find my hand being grasped in a firm handshake. Once again I am struck by his compact frame. It seems difficult to imagine this slim unshaven man with tousled hair standing in front of me is the same good-looking guy packing them in with his three-legged kicks and fists of fury.[18] (He explains later that he prefers to keep a mustache when he is not filming. The current mustache is only three days old).

But even millionaire actors have to work, and Bruce Lee tears himself away to begin the dubbing of special sound effects for his film, *The Way of the Dragon*. The film was shot in Rome and they have just completed putting in the dialogue. For the next four to five days he will be supervising the improvisation of the special sound effects—footsteps, cats calling and things like that.

We take a short walk to the recording studio and it soon becomes obvious that this idol of thousands in Asia is an extremely friendly person. Each of the studio hands we pass by is greeted with a "good morning" or "how are you today?" "How is the work?" he calls out to a man walking hurriedly past. The man looks up and Bruce Lee realizes that he has mistaken the man for somebody else. "Sorry, case of mistaken identity, but good morning all the same," he shouts out in Cantonese.

The five workers who are responsible for providing the special sound effects for the new film are already assembled when we arrive at the studio at 9:50 AM. He introduces me to his assistant, Mr. Chik Yiu Cheung, but leaves the rest to introduce themselves. "Excuse me a moment," says Bruce Lee, "I have to look for my towel. I can't adapt myself to this terrible heat. Give me the cold anytime."

He leaves the group, taking off his beige shirt at the same time. But he is back within five minutes wanting to know who will be providing the rumbling sound of an empty stomach required in one of the first scenes of the film. "Who's hungry?" he asks. "We'll bring the microphone to his stomach to record it." But everyone apparently has had a hearty breakfast and nobody is hungry. So he decides to put off the scene for the moment and start with something else.

Turning to me Bruce Lee says: "This is the first time that I have directed a film, and on the whole I must say I am satisfied with the result. Nevertheless there is, of course, still room for improvement. I read lots of books on cinematography and I know what I want. I tell the camera man what I have in mind, but I usually leave the technical work to him. I have to admit that I am no specialist. What do I think is good directing? Well, I think a good director should give the audience the feeling that there is no director behind the action at all. It must be real and natural."

He breaks off his discourse at this point as a red light comes on just then. Everyone in the room holds his breath as the sounds for a few scenes are recorded. But the scenes have to be redone because a radio is playing in the background. One of the workers explains that the buildings next to the studio are occupied by squatters and they cannot do anything about the interference. "Okay," Bruce Lee says in Cantonese, "get me some men and we will clear the whole lot out in no time." Everybody laughs in jest. The radio owner must also have heard his suggestion and taken it seriously for the set grows silent, and the dubbing carries on.

This actor, whose last film, *Fist of Fury,* has grossed more than $800,000 in Singapore alone, $2.2 million in the British colony, and $760,000 in Taiwan, decides to tell me about the film which he has just completed directing. "I really don't want to appear to be bragging," he says. "But I am confident that this film will do even better than the other two. I wrote the script and I play a Kowloon boy who is asked to go to Rome to help out a relative in trouble. The relative runs a Chinese restaurant, but is being pressured into selling the restaurant by some hoodlums. The climax takes place in the famous Coliseum in Rome and I have to fight an American who has won the karate championship in the States seven times!"

The central character, whose name means Dragon in English—hence the title, *The Way of the Dragon*—is a little like The Big Boss and Chen Chen in *Fist of Fury*, but he is also slightly different. "He is a simple man like [the character I played in] *The Big Boss*, but he likes to act big, you see. He doesn't really understand a metropolis like Rome, but he pretends that he does. He doesn't want to appear the country bumpkin, so rather than admit his ignorance of the language to the Italian waitress, he merely points to the menu to order. The result is he ends up drinking five bowls of soup."

At this point, Bruce Lee's sharp black eyes catch sight of one of the workers massaging the neck of a woman colleague. "Let me do it," he volunteers. Again without waiting for an answer—not that I think the girl would have refused—the director starts kneading her back and shoulders with the air of a professional. He obviously knows what he is doing too, for a few minutes later the woman claims that she is feeling much better.

So we return to our interrupted conversation. How does he write his script, I wanted to know. Does he write in English or Chinese? He speaks excellent English when talking to me and Cantonese to his colleagues in the movie industry. "I write in Chinese and get somebody else to polish it up a bit," he says with remarkable frankness. "I tried writing it in English at first and to have somebody translate it into Chinese, but it didn't work. The translation inevitably loses some of the original ideas. So I decided to write in Chinese with the help of a dictionary. It is quite funny really. I bought this English-Chinese dictionary originally to help me find the suitable English words when I first went to the United States when I was 18. Now I find that I have to use it to find the Chinese words which I have in mind."

Although the actor was born in San Francisco he spent most of his early life in Hong Kong and only returned to the U.S. when he was 18 to enter college. It is nearing noon now and the sound effects people have gone out of the studio to tape some moving traffic for a street scene. The place is quiet and Bruce Lee, who has not kept still longer than 10 minutes since I've seen him this morning, decides to read Alex Josey's column in *New Nation* about Bruce Lee's last film shown in Singapore, *Fist of Fury*. As he continues to the end of the column it is apparent that he does not agree with it.

"He is viewing a Chinese film with a Westerner's mind," he says. "Have you seen the TV series 'All in the Family'? It is a success in the West, but it would be a complete disaster if you were to look at it purely from the Chinese viewpoint. I think we should try to see films according to the cultural background of the people the films are aimed at. I don't think Mr. Josey should call it a comedy. To the Chinese the humiliation felt in those years was real. There is nothing to laugh about."[19] He agrees, however, that there are certain sections in his films which he does not expect his audience to take too seriously.

I decide to change the subject, so we begin discussing his daily jogging. I ask to be allowed to take photographs of him jogging one of these mornings, but he refuses. "Jogging is not only a form of exercise to me," he says. "It is also a form of relaxation. It is my own hour every morning, when I can be alone with my own thoughts."

Now he decides to change the subject and starts whistling his favorite tune, "I'd Like To Teach the World To Sing." He breaks off suddenly and announces: "But if there is one thing I'm certain of, it is the fact that I can't sing. I tell people I have a rich voice—because it is well off."

By now the food has arrived in little boxes and he hands one to me. As we sit we talk about the two-handled weapon which he uses in *Fist of Fury* and which has become popular in Singapore as well as in Taiwan.[20] "Man, I had to use something, you know. After all that guy was coming for me with a sword!" he says. "And no man, certainly not I, can use bare fists against swords, so we had to think of a weapon for me. I used it once in 'The Green Hornet series.' The weapon probably originated in China, but later traveled to Okinawa and then Japan."

Asked if he contemplates acting in a sword-fighting drama

one of these days, he replies in the affirmative. Provided he has the right script, he would like to act in a period film. He finishes lunch and announces that he must ring home to find out how his wife is doing. They have just bought a new house and are still in the process of settling in. He finds that he has forgotten the telephone number, however, and has to look up his notebook for it.

By 1:30 PM everyone is back at work and I decide not to ask any questions but to play the role of an observer. At the first break the woman worker suggests that one of her colleagues buy her a drink. The alert Bruce Lee hears it and immediately offers to buy drinks for all. Some cakes are also ordered, but when I refuse one, saying that it was too soon after lunch, he suggests that I should take it as dessert. Logical, I guess, since it is still too early for tea.

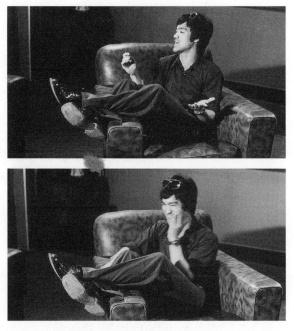

"It soon becomes obvious that this idol of thousands in Asia is an extremely friendly person," Pang Cheng Lian wrote about Bruce Lee, seen here enjoying himself on the set at Golden Harvest Studios in Hong Kong.

At the next break, one of his friends decides to test his reflexes. He is asked to try and catch a dollar note as it slips from a hand. He has to place his hand just under that of the man holding the note, but he cannot move his hand to catch it as it falls. The first few times the note moves too fast for his hand, but he soon gets the hang of it.

He decides to give some pointers on fighting to a few of his friends who have come in to watch him. "You must be fierce, but have patience at the same time," he counsels. "Most important of all, you must have complete determination. The worst opponent you can come across is one whose aim has become an obsession. For instance if a man has decided that he is going to bite off your nose no matter what happens to him in the process, the chances are he will succeed in doing it. He may be severely beaten up too, but that will not stop him from carrying out his objective. That is the real fighter. Women fighters? They are all right, but they are no match for the men who are physiologically stronger, except for a few vulnerable points. My advice is that if they have to fight, hit the man at his vital spots and then run. Women are more likely to achieve their objectives through feminine wiles and persuasion."

At this juncture the red light comes on again and the sound effects workers concentrate to provide the sounds created by Bruce Lee while sparring on his own. Remember those loud crackling sounds you heard in his first two films, every time he exhibited his flying kicks? Bruce Lee gets interested in the way they provide the sound effects—wild horses will not make me reveal how they are achieved—and in a few minutes he is joining the sound effects gang.

By this time the man who operates the movie projector breaks off for a snack so work is again stopped. Somebody in the room starts talking about the "accessibility" of a particular actress. But Bruce Lee, who appears angry for the first time, immediately defends her. "People in Hong Kong gossip too much," he snaps. "How do they know which actress is available and which isn't? People have nothing to do so they start weaving such stories about the different actresses, without realizing the harm they are causing." Before he can continue with his strong views, the man handling the projector has finished his snack and the red light signaling for silence is on again.

At the next break, one of his friends, who acted with him in *The Big Boss*, asks his advice on a business card he has just had printed. The young man is starting a karate class, but the printer has put under his name "Director and Chief Instructor of Self-Defiance Agency." "Self-Defiance"?, Bruce Lee laughs loudly. He goes on to explain in Cantonese to his friend the difference between self-defense and self-defiance. For the next half an hour he is involved in correcting the business card.

At 4:15 PM a photographer from one of the Hong Kong papers walks into the room. He starts taking shots of Bruce Lee and wants to know whether it is true that he will be acting for Shaw Brothers. "If they have a good script, I will consider it," Bruce Lee replies. "I want to be neutral and act for whichever company can provide me with the good scripts. I don't want to be involved in any conflicts or competition here."

Within a short space of time another five photographers attached to Hong Kong newspapers appear on the scene, asking the same question—has Bruce Lee agreed to act for Shaws? By this time he is just a little irritated and he replies: "Tell them I've signed for 20 films with Shaws." Then he leaves the group and goes to another corner of the room, seemingly to do some bending exercises. The photographers leave soon after.

The group breaks up, but actor-turned-director Bruce Lee promises to see me for a longer interview another day.

II. He has special plans to win worldwide fame

Having taken Asia by storm, Bruce Lee Hsiao Loong plans to win world fame. He will be the first Chinese actor to play the leading role in an American film.

Bruce Lee, the San Francisco-born Chinese actor who has thrilled millions in Asia through his pugilistic skills, will be starring in a joint production with Warner Brothers of the U.S.[21]

The Chinese movie phenomenon who shot to fame in his first Chinese film, revealed that agreement has already been reached between him and Warner Brothers regarding a joint production. The American partner is now preparing a script for the film in which Bruce Lee will play the leading role.

"The script is the most important thing," he said. "That is why

I have always insisted on having a good script before accepting the role. Just recently I turned down a Golden Harvest film because I wasn't happy with the script.[22] At present I am working on the script for my next film. I haven't really decided on the title yet, but what I want to show is the necessity to adapt oneself to changing circumstances. The inability to adapt brings destruction.[23]

"I already have the first scene in my mind. As the film opens, the audience sees a wide expanse of snow. Then the camera closes in on a clump of trees while the sounds of a strong gale fill the screen. There is a huge tree in the center of the screen and it is all covered with thick snow. Suddenly there is a loud snap and a huge branch of the tree falls to the ground. It cannot yield to the force of the snow so it breaks. Then the camera moves to a willow tree which is bending with the wind. Because it adapts itself to the environment, the willow survives.[24] It is this sort of symbolism which I think Chinese action films should seek to have.

"In this way I hope to broaden the scope of action films. The box-office success of my first two films for Golden Harvest has given me a certain amount of maneuverability. I can do what I like usually in the film. But it has also set certain limitations. People expect me to fight, you know. They expect action from me. So in a way I am imprisoned by my own success too."

Of late, I pointed out, there have been complaints that there is too much violence in Chinese films. What does he think of such complaints? "I do not believe in playing up violence," said the man who owes his popularity to his fine display of martial arts on celluloid. "I think it is unhealthy to play up violence. If a man has his throat slit during a fight for example, the audience should not be given a frontal view of his blood-soaked throat. But it should be remembered that violence and aggression is part of everyday life now. You see it over the TV and in Vietnam. You can't just pretend that it does not exist. On the other hand, I don't think one should use violence and aggression as themes of movies. The glorification of violence is bad. That is why I insisted that Chen Chen, the role I played in *Fist of Fury*, should die in the film. He had killed many people and he had to pay for it."

Despite the tremendous box-office success of his first two Chinese films—the second, *Fist of Fury*, has broken records in Hong Kong, Taiwan and Singapore—Bruce Lee is surprisingly critical of both. Both, he thought, have plenty of room for improvement if they are to win international appeal.

But, I argued, I understand that Golden Harvest is now dubbing *The Big Boss* in English for general screening in London and Australia. "Yes," he agreed, "Raymond, the producer, is keen on the idea, but I'm personally not too happy. And it is not only the production, but the theme that I am talking about.

"You see, there is a cultural gap between the West and the East. What is good for the Westerners may not necessarily be good for the Easterners and vice versa. Learning English for example, is not too difficult. But to understand the nuances of tones and the meaning of colloquial expressions—that is difficult. At present, most of our Chinese films are geared towards the South-East Asian audience. People here have different tastes from those of people who live in the West. We have to try and produce films with universal appeal if we are to gain international recognition. This is what I intend to achieve in my future films. *The Way of the Dragon*, the film I've just finished directing and acting in, is only the beginning."

But the cultural gap is not the only barrier against Chinese films seeking international appreciation. Bruce Lee indicated that the inferior quality of production is another factor. Those involved in the movie industry, he thought, were not professional enough.

"Take today for example," he said. "Everyone knows that we start work at nine. It is 9:30 AM now. The director, myself, is here, but my workers have not arrived. This sort of thing is unheard of in the States. Part of the reason these people are late is that it is the fashion for other directors and big stars to be late. The other problem about the Hong Kong film industry is that there are too many stars and too few actors. Box-office popularity often provides the stars with considerable power. Unfortunately, many tend to misuse it."

Success, according to the new wonder-man of the Hong Kong film industry, is not without its pitfalls. He explained: "There are too many temptations. Recently, for instance, I was offered HK $250,000 to appear for a few moments in a commercial. There are also many movie offers but I feel that it would not be fair to anyone if I start shooting a dozen films a year. I can't possibly give any of the films the full attention and concentration that it requires. I want to limit the number of films which I appear in each year. These tempting offers are making life more and more complicated."

If rumors are true, the offers are indeed tempting. People in the film industry are speculating that some producers are prepared to pay him a million Hong Kong dollars for a film. Bruce Lee was quite candid about the importance of money. "Sure money is important in providing for my family and giving us what we want. But it isn't everything," he said.

Bruce Lee, it appears, is not a great money-spender. He does not smoke, drink or gamble. "I don't think putting smoke into your body is quite the thing to do," he said. "As for alcohol, I think it tastes awful. Don't know why anyone should want to drink the stuff. As for gambling, I don't believe in getting something for nothing. But I do buy lots of clothes although I seldom have the chance to show them off, since I go out very infrequently."

The actor, script-writer and director has little interest in social engagements or publicity appearances. He prefers to spend his free time with his wife and two children, and only goes out occasionally with some close friends. Since we were on the subject of his likes and dislikes, I decided to ask him to name a few more examples. "Oh, I like light rain," he said. "It gives one such a sense of calmness and tranquillity. I enjoy walking in the rain. But most of all, I like books. I read all types of books—fiction and non-fiction. What I detest most is dishonest people who talk more than they are capable of doing. I also mind people who use false humility as a means to cover their obnoxious inadequacy."

Being an extremely frank man by nature, and perhaps influenced by his long stay in the U.S., Bruce Lee admits that he opens to people enthusiastically. But he finds that people in Hong Kong tend to be more guarded. "Then there is the other group of people who try to utilize me for their own ends," he said. "There was this producer who insisted that I go along to see the rushes of his new film. To oblige him I did. The next thing I knew, advertisements for the film proclaimed in bold print that Bruce Lee had spoken highly of the production!"

To my surprise, Bruce Lee revealed that though his rise to fame in the film industry has been quite recent and sudden, his association with movies has been very long. His first appearance on the screen took place when he was only three months old; in a Chinese film produced in San Francisco. He starred in several Cantonese films in his teens when he was living in Hong Kong.

The last film he appeared in before leaving for the U.S. in his late teens was probably his best known, entitled *The Orphan*. For the part he received HK $1,000—which is estimated to be worth about HK $3,500 today—not a bad salary in those days.

Thug

In the U.S. Bruce Lee's martial skill won him the role of Kato in "The Green Hornet" TV series. As Kato, he played the faithful friend and companion of Britt Reid, the crusading crime-busting newspaperman who adopts the guise of the Green Hornet in his fight against crime and corruption.

In the late sixties, he played a small part as a thug in Metro-Goldwyn-Mayer's production of *Marlowe*, a detective thriller. Then early this year he played the title role in *The Big Boss*, a Golden Harvest production, and Bruce Lee has not looked back since. How does he explain his fantastic rise to fame?

"My 12 years of preparation in the States," was his prompt reply. "Without them I would be little different from the others here. I was in the U.S. in my formative years and I think I learned a lot there. Another important factor is the great interest I have in my work. I am willing to give 101 percent attention to my films. Partly, I suppose, the audience senses the animalism in me."

The actor whose two films are currently the biggest money-makers among Chinese movies claims that breaking box-office records does not mean very much to him. "The important thing is that I am personally satisfied with my work," he said. "If it is a piece of junk, I will only regret it."

Bruce Lee waves to appreciative fans after a television appearance in Hong Kong to promote his third film The Way of the Dragon. His hope was that the film would "show the necessity to adapt oneself to changing circumstances. The inability to adapt brings destruction." He accomplished his objective in his brilliant fight choreography for the film's climactic battle with American martial artist Chuck Norris.

But what of his future plans? "Well, I want to direct more films," he said quickly. "Directing, I feel, is more creative. You really get a chance to produce the result you want. An actor is restricted. He can only do as the director instructs. In my case I can influence the production to a certain extent because of my present status. But it is not a satisfactory state of affairs because I know I am interfering and I hate to interfere with other people's work."

The self-confident actor who has just finished directing his first film sets no limit to his career. "One must always strive to be better," he said. "The sky's the limit."

He does feel, however, that a man's fighting days are over when he reaches 45. "The man himself will not realize it and will probably deny it," he said. "But physiologically, he is already on the decline and I think the fighter over 45 should sit back and watch the emergence of the new ones."

And Bruce Lee, 31, should know what he is talking about for he has been studying martial arts since the age of 13. He has even founded his own school called Jeet Kune Do. A strict definition of Jeet Kune Do, however, is difficult to come by since the founder Bruce Lee stresses change and adaptability. He believes that the true martial arts teacher should help the student to "discover" for himself the best style of fighting most suited to him.

The former Jeet Kune Do instructor—he no longer has any time to do any teaching for obvious reasons—is against mass education of students along strict traditional methods. Instead, he is of the opinion that they have to explore and discover for themselves what comes more naturally. It was his refusal to follow the trend of popularizing martial arts in the U.S. which made him close his three schools in Seattle, Oakland and Los Angeles a few years ago.[25]

"Not every man can take lessons to be a good fighter," he said. "He must be a person who is able to relate his training to the circumstances he encounters. "Self-actualization is the important thing. And my personal message to people is that I hope they will go towards self-actualization rather than self-image actualization. I hope that they will search within themselves for honest self-expression."

III. Success has not gone to his head, says his wife

Linda Lee, the blue-eyed blonde from Seattle is probably the only one in the world who is not surprised by Bruce Lee's phenomenal success. "I knew all along that he had it in him. The only difference is that others are aware of it now," she said over lunch last week.

Which is really not a surprising statement, I guess, since American-born Linda ("I have some Swedish blood on my mother's side") is the wife of Bruce Lee, the man who rates as one of the most popular Chinese actors in Asia today.

They have been married for nine years and only the blind will fail to see that they are greatly attached to one another.

Soft-spoken Linda was at first reluctant to be interviewed—"We prefer to separate his family from his career," I was told—but as we proceed from onion soup to pepper steak, it becomes pretty clear that she was very enthusiastic about discussing her husband, Bruce Lee.

"He is not the sort of person who pays a great deal of attention to ceremony and form," she said. "For example, he thinks that opening doors or bringing flowers are unimportant things. These are merely actions; it is the thought that you have for a person which is important. But he is very considerate. He always remembers birthdays and anniversaries. He has got the knack of getting along with people. He makes friends easily, but he can read people better than I can. I think I am more gullible and tend to take people at face value, but Bruce can make very accurate assessments of people's characters at first meetings."

Nothing like getting the story from the beginning, I thought, so I asked Linda how she met and married Bruce Lee, the Chinese from Hong Kong. "We met in Seattle," she said. "We were both studying at the University of Washington, although he was a year my senior. He was doing philosophy while I wanted to do medicine. We actually met through his martial arts class. You see, he had started a school in Seattle as a part-time job, and I had a Chinese girl-friend who had enrolled in his school. We all thought it was quite funny about her taking 'kung fu' at first, but I decided to go along and have a look one day. That was how I met Bruce. I got interested in the class and decided to enroll. No, I don't think that I enrolled primarily because I wanted to get to know him," she added in reply to my query.

She went on: "A Hong Kong magazine reporter once asked me

whether I had fallen in love with Bruce first or whether he had made the first move. I said I did. Women normally have more love to give. Don't you agree? Anyway, we started dating but we didn't really think seriously of marriage until he decided to move to Oakland. He asked if I wanted to go with him. I thought for exactly 30 seconds and I accepted the proposal."

How did your parents take it, I asked. After all, though Bruce Lee was born in the States, he is a Chinese. Did your parents object? "My father's dead, and my mother wasn't too happy about my marrying so young," she replied with disarming frankness. "I was the younger of two daughters and my sister had already got married. I was doing well in my studies and my mother was hoping that I would finish medical school at least before settling down. Mother wasn't against Bruce because he was a Chinese although she did worry that I might suffer racial discrimination from others. But her fears proved to be unfounded. Everyone was extremely nice to us and I didn't think we experienced it at all. Partly, I guess, because Bruce is a very easy person to get along with."

I asked if success has made Bruce Lee difficult to live with, but Linda at once squashed the suggestion. "Oh no, he hasn't changed at all," she said. "Of course we get recognized in the streets nowadays and he receives scores of fan mail (but he was already receiving them when he was doing his "Green Hornet" series). However, once we are together in our home everything is the same. His overnight success hasn't changed him one bit. He still prefers to spend most of his free time with his family. We usually stay at home. Now that we have bought this new house we will have even less need to get out."

Located in Kowloon, Bruce Lee's new house is palatial with eight bedrooms covering more than 12,000 sq. ft. and estimated to be worth $750,000. But Bruce Lee's busy filming schedule also means that he has to spend long working hours out of the house. "Sometimes I don't see him for days on end," she says wistfully. "But then there will be other days when he is completely free and the family is together. Personally, I wouldn't want it any other way. I don't think I would like him to have a steady nine to five job."

She values his company so much that she has put off a plan to attend regular Chinese classes at the Asia College.

What about plans to join the movie industry herself? "I don't think it will be a good idea at the moment," she said. "I think Bruce prefers me as I am now. Right now I want to learn Cantonese quickly. He discusses his ideas with his friends in Cantonese and I want to be able to understand and join in the discussions."

Linda believes that a successful marriage is one in which the two partners should have similar as well as different interests. In her case the similar interests are Bruce Lee's career and a love for reading. She added that at the moment she is more interested in reading books on China and Chinese art, Chinese people and the Chinese way of life. She has just finished reading an autobiography of Han Suyin. With great candor she admitted that she does not sew, "except for pajamas and housecoats which do not need to fit well." Most of her clothes are bought off the peg "because Hong Kong tailors are so expensive and a really good one is hard to find."

As for woman's lib, she is all for equal pay for equal work for women, but is against the militant aspects of the movement. Finally, we began to discuss a very basic feminine emotion—jealousy. How does she feel when she sees her husband in the arms of another woman on the screen? "It doesn't bother me one bit," she said with a laugh. "It is difficult to feel romantic you know when you are acting a scene in front of a camera and under the blaze of those powerful lights. It is only part of his job as an actor. We do have laughs over them. For instance, when we were watching his film, *The Big Boss,* there was a scene where Bruce faces a nude prostitute. He leaned over and whispered to me, 'Part of the fringe benefits.' That is how we take it."

Coffee had been served by then and we ended the interview. I was convinced that with an intelligent and sensible wife like Linda, it is no wonder that Bruce Lee considers her "his better half."

What He Thinks of His Wife

Linda Lee's boundless enthusiasm for Bruce Lee is only exceeded by his tremendous feelings for her. For, in his own words: "My wife is the luckiest thing that ever happened to me—not *The Big Boss*."

The good-looking actor whom hundreds of girls would give their right arm for—one told a taximan that she was prepared to be his ninth concubine—went on to explain his great admiration for his wife. "The important thing is that she understands me," he said. "I'm a loner by nature and she lets me be what I am. That is not easy. When I am down she doesn't try to overwhelm me with sympathy or make useless clucking noises as other women are prone to do. When I am happy, she shares my joy. The other great thing about her is that she hasn't changed one bit in spite of my success."(Linda had used the very same words to describe him). "Wives of other great stars here start putting on airs and playing mahjong. But Linda is still the same as before."

But while he is ever-ready to sing his wife's praises, Bruce Lee insists on keeping his family life separate from his career. Once he finishes his work, he prefers to spend his leisure with Linda and their two lively children, Brandon, 7, and Shannon, 3. "When Linda was pregnant the first time I was quite confident that it was going to be a boy," he said with pride. "We only chose a boy's name for the unborn baby. We didn't even bother thinking of a girl's name." Sure enough Linda had a boy—8 lb, 11 oz Brandon. "The second time I had decided it was going to be a girl, so we only chose a girl's name. And we had Shannon."

He is absolutely happy with his two bundles of joy and has no plans to have more. Like all parents the world over, Bruce Lee is immensely proud of his two children, particularly Brandon whom he once described as "a blond-haired, grey-eyed Chinaman."

Next month Brandon will be starting his second year in a school in Hong Kong which teaches in English as well as Chinese. Having lived in the U.S. for most of his life, Brandon's Chinese is a little weak and he has to have private tuition in the language. Right now the little man is not too cheerful for his parents have insisted that tuition will continue during the summer vacation.

Bruce Lee makes no bones about how proud he is of Brandon. He declared: "Brandon takes after me. He is full of energy, always running around and never sitting still for a minute."

Young Brandon has the makings of a good fighter too. A few weeks ago when the whole Lee family appeared in a Hong Kong TV show for charity, the seven year old boy thrilled viewers by breaking two one-inch planks with a side kick. He has been practicing with his father since he was two, but Bruce Lee is against regular lessons for the moment because he feels that Brandon is still too young.

Shannon, the baby in the family, will be starting nursery school in September. She is probably too young to understand and probably wonders what all the fuss over her father is about.

Bruce Lee himself is the fourth child in a family of five. His father, a well-known Cantonese opera actor, Lee Hoi Chuen, is dead, while his mother lives in Los Angeles with his younger brother, Robert, who is now studying computer science. His two sisters are married while his elder brother, who holds a masters degree in physics and mathematics, is working in the Royal Observatory in Hong Kong. His brother has won a fencing championship in the British colony.

Until this year Bruce Lee and Linda were living in a 2,000 sq. ft. house in Los Angeles. They had originally planned to stay in the States and to fly to Hong Kong only for his filming. But the fantastic success of his second film, *Fist of Fury*, convinced him that his immediate future lay in the Chinese movie industry and the family decided to make Hong Kong their home base. Bruce, his wife and children moved into their new house early this month.

Bruce Lee has his own study in the house—for reading and writing more movie scripts—and is planning to build a gym where he can spar with his close friends.

Off Duty/Pacific, November 1972

SUPERSTAR BRUCE LEE?

Who's he? Well, he's to "Easterns" what ol' John Wayne was to Westerns

by Jack Moore

You ever wondered what philosophy students do for a living, once they get out of school? Well, one of them, a young man named Bruce Lee, who majored in the metaphysical at the University of Washington, has made out just fine, thank you. Mixing Western philosophical thought and Eastern philosophical training, he has become the biggest star in the East. Lee, who is built like the Great Wall of China, is to Chinese Easterns what John Wayne used to be to Westerns.

You may have seen him several times, if you go to a lot of movies or keep up with Stateside TV. And if you appreciate Chinese movies, you probably have already booked your tickets to his next film.

At the age of 32, he is something of a trans-Pacific Man. When he's not in Hong Kong, making buckets of money starring in Mandarin-language productions, he's in Hollywood, playing support roles and trying to break into the front ranks of American cinema and television stars. It's a frustrating sort of life that could give a lesser-willed man a split personality.

"Sometimes I feel a little schizophrenic about it," Lee says. "When I wake up in the morning, I have to remember which side of the ocean I'm on, and whether I'm the superstar or the exotic Oriental support player."

The confusion is easier to handle, he admits, if you're a man with a Western wife and two Sino-American children, one of which Lee describes as "a fantastic little seven-year-old brown-haired, blue-eyed Chinaman."

Still, he has been back and forth across that ocean enough times to make Ferdinand Magellan green with envy, and there's no end in sight.

"I was born in Hong Kong and spent my childhood here," he said.[26] "My father was a comedian and opera star, and my brother Robert was into music, but aside from a few child-actor roles in Cantonese movies, I wasn't the show business sort.

"What I was really interested in was self-defense. We Chinese have been perfecting methods of armed and unarmed combat for thousands of years, and the study of martial arts is a venerable and respected one. It is also very handy if you happen to live in a tough neighborhood, like I did."

He continued his fist-fighting studies after the family moved to the United States and he became an American citizen.[27] After he left the university in Seattle, he opened a self-defense school. It was highly popular, and before long he had a chain of three of them, in Seattle, Oakland and Los Angeles. "It was a very profitable thing to do," he said. "I used to charge $500 for a 10-hour course, and people flocked to the schools. I even doubled the price, and people still kept coming. I had no idea so many Americans were interested in Chinese boxing."

He says that he would cheerfully go back to being a boxing instructor (at those rates, who wouldn't?) if his current show-business career ever packs up. But that, he admits with a small smile, doesn't seem likely just at the moment.

The film career began at his Los Angeles school, where he found himself teaching the likes of Steve McQueen, James Coburn, Lee Marvin and James Garner. The influence of these clients, plus the fact that he was "discovered" at an international karate tournament in Long Beach in 1964, led to his first American screen part.

"Naturally, I was signed to play Charlie Chan's Number One

Son. I mean, that's what Chinese actors do for a living in Holly-wood, isn't it? Charlie himself is always played by a round-eye wear-ing six pounds of makeup. Anyway, the Charlie Chan movie never got made, and I was signed to do some 'Batman' bits for television. And then came my first steady part—as Kato, on 'The Green Hor-net' series. You know why I got the job playing Kato?" he asks, going into a "routine." "I'll tell you why I got the job playing Kato. I got the job playing Kato because the hero's name was Britt Reid, and I was the only Chinese guy in all of California who could pronounce 'Britt Reid,' that's why. Anyway, it was fun, and it put my foot in a lot of important doorways in Hollywood. Among other things, it led to my first movie part."

The part was in a movie called *Marlowe*, which starred James Garner. Lee played a Chinese heavy named Winslow Wong, and Garner got to dispose of his old boxing tutor by heaving him off a rooftop. Sort of a messy way to go, Lee admits, but a very nice way to break into Hollywood movies. And then came another television part, and one that Lee says is the most important bit of English-lan-guage acting he's ever done, far more important and difficult than the "Batman" and "The Green Hornet" bits.

"It was in a series called 'Longstreet' and I played a Chinese boxing instructor (what else?) who was grooming this blind dude for a very important street fight. James Franciscus played the blind hero, and I had this really wonderful piece of Stirling Silliphant script to work from. That man is the greatest screenwriter of all time. He wrote me a really beautiful monologue. You want to hear it? Lis-ten…" (At this point, Lee assumes a far-away expression and every-one in the room shuts up and listens. He is one hell of a good actor.)

> Listen, man, you can't see but you can HEAR. Listen to the wind. The WIND! Listen to the birds. Can you hear them? You have to BECOME the wind. Empty your mind, man. You know how water fills a cup? It BECOMES that cup. You have to be ready, man. You have to think about nothing. You have to be-come fluid. You have to BECOME nothing.

Gorgeous stuff, it was, and enough to start some TV executives thinking about a series with Lee as the star. It was to have been called "The Warrior," and feature Lee as a Chinese knight who somehow wandered into the American West and hassled with cowboys, Indians and so on. It was a far-out idea, but some people were a little worried that a Chinese hero might not go over very well in parts of the United States. "They didn't know if people were ready for Hopalong Wong," says Lee wryly.

The series eventually became one 90-minute special [which later became a prime-time hit called "Kung Fu," starring Caucasian actor, David Carradine—Ed.], which is due to be aired sometime around the end of this year. In the meantime, back on the coast of China, the Mandarin movie world had experienced a big split. Cantonese-language films had stopped being produced, the Mandarin industry had been taken over by Shaw Brothers, a huge international complex run by a single family, and independent producers were looking for something to replace the endless swordfighting flicks that were the standard Saturday-afternoon-at-the movies fare for Chinese cinemagoers.

One of the producers, a man named Raymond Chow, heard about Lee and decided to offer him a contract and risk a lot of money on a gigantic one-shot Chinese boxing movie. Even with Hong Kong's low-cost movie operations, it ran up a bill of $100,000—big by Hong Kong standards—and Chow was hoping desperately that he would make it back. Lee, who flew over from Los Angeles to make the film, now says he thought it would and a small profit to boot.

Neither of them expected the incredible crush at the box-office that followed. Before the film opened on a commercial basis there were five special midnight previews, and there wasn't an empty seat in the house. The film was called *The Big Boss*, and was set in Thailand. After a mere 19 days on the screens of Hong Kong, alone, it had grossed close to $600,000, and had broken the colony's all-time box-office record set in 1966 by *The Sound of*

Music. More than one and a quarter million people saw it during its first run.

Bruce Lee was a superstar. (Or rather Lee Siu-lung was—that's the name Chinese movie fans know him by—Bruce Lee was still trying to make it big back there in the States.)

"We immediately began plans for a second film," Lee says. It was titled *Fist of Fury*, and this time, the box-office closed at nearly $800,000. Currently, work is being completed on a third, to be called *The Way of the Dragon*. "This one I wrote and directed as well," Lee says. This one, Lee figures, will top the $1 million mark.

Part of Lee's success undoubtedly is due to the strong xenophobia he arouses in his Chinese audiences. A Western friend of mine tells of going to see *Fist of Fury* when it opened in Hong Kong. The setting of the story is Shanghai in the 1920s, when China was a pitiful figure in world politics. Through unfair treaties imposed upon her, many foreign powers held "concessions" that gave them control over large sectors of the economy and free reign to exploit practically at will.

In the movie, Lee plays the role of (what else?) a young assistant instructor in a Chinese boxing school. One day some Japanese come to the school, humiliate Bruce's master and proceed to wreck the place. Bitter with hatred, and intent on revenge, Lee retreats to the forest and embarks on a rigorous and grueling program of physical conditioning. Finally, after months of intense, dedicated training he is ready for his revenge. He goes to the Japanese's own karate school and, KAPOW! OOMPHH! KAZOWIE! he proceeds to wipe the floor with the pride of the Nipponese knuckle academy. Standing in the midst of the desolation he has wreaked, savoring the moment to the fullest, Lee turns full to the camera and says these words, very slowly and deliberately:

"Now you know...Chinese are no longer the sick men of Asia!"

The effect was about like striking up "Dixie" at a Klu Klux Klan rally. A mighty roar, deafening applause and stamping of feet shook the theater. My Western friend scrunched lower in his seat, suddenly feeling very much the foreigner in an alien land.

Exactly how much Lee gets out of these films is his little secret, but it's bound to be a lot. When you consider that Mandarin movies are made in six weeks, that these films will be grossing money from re-runs for the next Confucius-knows-how-many years, and that there is no end in sight to Lee's popularity, this makes him one of the most comfortable people in the entertainment business.

His only problem these days is time. He says he finds himself dashing back and forth between Los Angeles (where the opportunities are) and Hong Kong (where the money is) four and five times a year.

"It's a very schizophrenic way to make a living, but then, that's what University of Washington philosophy courses prepare you for, I suppose."

The Hong Kong Standard, February 10, 1973

THE VIOLENCE CULT

by Piera Kwan

It looks as if the film industry in Southeast Asia has found its savior in the person of Bruce Lee, the much talked-about fighter-actor of Mandarin films. Over a plate of Australian rock oysters, the confident 32-year-old star sold himself hard on the role, as we meandered through the size and shape of film art.

"I'm dissatisfied with the expression of cinematic art here in Hong Kong. That's why I decided to improve the situation and take up the making of *The Way of the Dragon.* And I did it on guts. I wouldn't have done it in the United States because they have enough competent directors, and I am not a professional. But it is time somebody did something about the films here. There are simply not enough soulful characters who are committed, dedicated and are at the same time professionals. I believe that I have a role here in Southeast Asia. The audience needs to be educated and the one to educate them has to be somebody who is responsible. We are dealing with the masses and we have to create some-

I believe that I have a role here in Southeast Asia. The audience needs to be educated and the one to educate them has to be somebody who is responsible. We are dealing with the masses and we have to create something that will get through to them. We have to educate them step by step. We can't do it overnight. That's what I am doing right now. Whether I succeed or not remains to be seen. But I don't just feel *committed, I am* committed.

thing that will get through to them. We have to educate them step by step. We can't do it overnight. That's what I am doing right now. Whether I succeed or not remains to be seen. But I don't just *feel* committed, I *am* committed," says Bruce Lee emphatically.

Film Contracts

"I can have all the film contracts I want, up to 1974, but I don't. This is the indication of an artist, because money isn't everything." It is undeniable that the films he has made continue to rake in fortunes for him and his foresighted backers. "It is an unfortunate fact but still a cold fact that cinema is a marriage of business and art, in Hollywood or Hong Kong. But I don't mind the money coming my way." He laughs softly.

Violence seems to have played a dominant role in the films Bruce Lee has acted in and perhaps to a slightly lesser extent in his directorial debut—The Way of the Dragon. When I voice this opinion, Bruce tries to put my mind at ease with a wave of his hand.

"I don't call the fighting in my films violence. I call it action. An action film borders somewhere between reality and fantasy. If I were to be completely realistic you would call me a bloody violent man. I would simply destroy my opponent by tearing him apart or ripping his guts out. I wouldn't do it so artistically. See, I have this intensity in me that the audience believes in what I do because I do believe in what I do."

He takes off his dark glasses and peers at me. "The intensity is there and I have to act in such a way as to border my action somewhere between reality and fantasy. As long as what I do is credible and as long as I have this intensity in me then all is well. I didn't create this monster—all this gore in the Mandarin films. It was there before I came. At least I don't spread violence. There is always justification for it. A man who has killed many people has to take responsibility for it. What I am trying to prove is that a man living by violence dies by violence."

Is it really necessary for us to be subjected to all this violence?

"But violence is there in our society. In a way, I perhaps anaesthetize violence by the way I move my body, so that the audience calls it not violence but body control. I never depend solely on my fighting skill to fulfill any of my film roles, although the audiences in Southeast Asia seem to think so. I believe it is more my personality and the expression of my body and myself. I am not acting, I am just doing my thing. When somebody tries to mimic my battle cries or grimaces he'd make himself look ridiculous."[28]

Is Mr. Lee suggesting he is a super-hero in all his films? "I don't play the super-hero. But the audience wants to make me one. I don't always play the same kind of role. Each role is different, although when I fight I come out the same—like an animal. There are two types of actors—the versatile one who can go from character to character, and then there is the kind who is type-cast, like Clint Eastwood, John Wayne and Charles Bronson. I see myself as lying somewhere between the two. I am a personality and each role I play shares a bit of that personality."

Presumably then, we can brace ourselves for Bruce's more diversified roles in the future, instead of the perpetual actor-fighter he has been so far?

"I would like to evolve into different roles, but I cannot do so in Southeast Asia. I am already type-cast. I am supposed to be the good guy. I can't even be a bit gray, because no producer would let me. Besides, I can't even express myself fully on film here, or the audience wouldn't understand what I am talking about half the time. That's why I can't stay in Southeast Asia all the time. I plan to stay half a year here and half a year in Hollywood. Right now I am doing a film for Warner Brothers.[29] I am responsible for a good part of the script, in collaboration with the director Bob Clouse. I have a hell of a responsibility because the Americans really do not have first-hand information on

"I have a hell of a responsibility because Americans really do not have first-hand information on the Chinese." Bruce Lee teaches a young student an aspect of Chinese philosophy in this scene from his blockbuster hit Enter the Dragon. Lee wrote this particular scene in an effort to share elements of Chinese culture with Americans.

the Chinese. The script has turned out to be a beauty, and artistic too."

He seems to have a child-like gleam in his eyes. "I am confident that my talent will expand internationally. I am improving and making new discoveries every day. If you don't you are already crystallized and that's it," says Bruce as he slashes his throat with his stiffly flattened hand.[30] "I will be doing different types of films in the future, some serious, some philosophical and some pure entertainment. But I will never prostitute myself in any way that I do what I don't believe in."

Bruce Lee's confidence leaves no doubt in my mind that he believes in his own charisma. But to catch a glimpse of the creative potential of our Mandarin film hero, we will have to look outside Southeast Asia for now.

The Hong Kong Years (1971–1973)

The China Mail, March 2, 1973

WHO WILL GET SUPERSTAR BRUCE LEE?

What will be Bruce Lee's next film after his first joint effort with Warner Brothers? The answer is still in doubt although the film, *Enter the Dragon,* is now nearing completion following weeks of shooting in town.

On the one hand, Shaws are trying to lure him into working under their banner for the first time at the earliest date possible.[31] A Shaw executive this week disclosed that a group of writers is now working on the script for the Bruce Lee film. He said it will be a modern action epic "to be made with great care" from April or May.[32] And Mr. Run Run Shaw even named the director Chor Yuen, who has been Bruce's close friend since childhood.

And, on the other, Shaw's opposition studio—Golden Harvest—intends to keep the superstar for their own productions. Mr. Raymond Chow confirmed that the studio is trying to bring together Bruce and former Cantonese film actress Siu Fong-fong, who's returning to the limelight in May. He said preliminary talks between both sides have so far turned out favorable.

Fong-fong, who's now in her last two months at Seton Hall University, New Jersey, will have her Mandarin film debut under Luk Bon's direction. It's a modern comedy.

The China Mail, March 16, 1973

BRUCE JUST TOO GOOD

Superstar Bruce Lee has been involved in a fight—and it proved a bit too much for his opponent. He floored a young man with a kick after the man had challenged his ability at the martial arts. It happened when Lee was filming an outdoor scene at Taitam Reservoir for his latest film, *Enter the Dragon.*

According to witnesses, the man, aged about 20, appeared suddenly on the set. He told Lee he had seen him perform a lot of Jeet Kune Do, a form of martial art, on the screen and wanted to see it in real life. The witness said the man sneered when Lee set himself in a stance— and that was too much for the actor. He lashed out with a kick and the man fell. When he recovered and seemed anxious to have a crack at Lee he was dragged away by several members of the camera crew.

About an altercation on the set of Enter the Dragon, *an observer reported: "He lashed out with a kick and the man fell." Bruce Lee on the set of that film, where at least one would-be tough guy found out the hard way that Lee's considerable ability in the martial arts was as impressive in life as it was on the screen.*

He was apparently uninjured, and refused to give his name. Onlookers thought he may have been a boxer from a local sect.[33]

The Star (Hong Kong), March 16, 1973

BRUCE FLOORS ACTOR

by Christine Chow

Film Superstar Bruce Lee yesterday floored a young part-time actor and almost knocked him unconscious during a filming session. The long-haired actor had challenged Lee to show him his boxing style. He had been watching the superstar making the movie *Enter the Dragon.*

This film is Lee's first attempt at an international release. According to reliable sources, the youth leapt from the sidelines and challenged Lee to a fight. Lee, angered at the youth's challenge, swung his fists at him and badly cut his mouth. He followed up with a kick which sent the youth sprawling on the ground, almost unconscious.

Film executive Raymond Chow today confirmed the incident but claimed it was "a friendly match.[34] The young man just wanted to see how Bruce fought, off the screen," he said. "It was just a little fight and there was no hard feelings between the two of them." Mr. Chow said filming resumed very quickly. He said the youth was a boxer who was appearing as a part-time actor in the movie.

Movie sources said it was the first time Lee had accepted a challenge from the many people who believe they could beat the superstar in a real fight. The youth's condition is satisfactory.

United Press International, July 20, 1973

ACTOR BRUCE LEE DIES IN HONG KONG HOSPITAL

HONG KONG—(UPI)—Bruce Lee, a one-time University of Washington student who parlayed his knowledge of Oriental martial arts into a movie career, died last night at Queen Elizabeth Hospital. He was 32.

The government information service said the cause of Lee's death was not immediately determined. He died shortly after admission to the hospital. Lee starred in numerous films made here featuring use of karate, Kung-fu and other martial arts. The films recently became popular internationally, particularly in the United States.

In Hollywood, Warner Bros. said Lee was born in San Francisco in 1940 of Chinese parents, raised in Hong Kong and at-

Bruce Lee—martial arts innovator, film pioneer, teacher, philosopher, husband, father, and friend. November 27, 1940–July 20, 1973.

tended the University of Washington, where he majored in philosophy. Lee then moved to Los Angeles with his wife, Linda, and apeared in a number of television roles.

Lee returned to Hong Kong where producer Raymond Chow starred him in *Fists of Fury* [sic], *The Big Boss* and *The Chinese Connection*—all featuring karate.[35] The films were made in Mandarin and dubbed in English. A film, *Enter the Dragon*, was made in English last Spring and is scheduled for release in August by Warner Bros.

Oct 1972

Bruce Lee is a man who only concentrates to make his script better. And only wants to make his movie better regardless of how much money it may cost. furthermore he cares for his family. And would drive himself day and night. Just to make his script better. He is always trying to make his film more lifelike and more dramatic. His movies are superb and my opinion of him is he is a hero, His films are so thrilling and

he is my idol. In America he would teach Yuet Kwoe Do and his students respected him

He is unable to walk down the streets without everyone asking for his autograph. He can be gentle even though at times he can be fierce. And he is quite happy with what he has achieved.

Brandon Bruce Lee,

THE FINAL WORD...

A little-known essay, written in October 1972 by Bruce Lee's seven-year-old son Brandon, published in Hong Kong prior to the release of The Way of the Dragon. *Brandon wrote:*

> *Bruce Lee is a man who only concentrates to make his script better. And only wants to make his movie better regardless of how much money it may cost. Furthermore he cares for his family. And would drive himself day and night, just to make his script better. He is always trying to make his film more lifelike and more dramatic. His movies are superb and my opinion of him is he is a hero. His films are so thrilling and he is my idol. In America he would teach Jeet Kune Do and his students respected him.*
>
> *He is unable to walk down the streets without everyone asking for his autograph. He can be gentle even though at times he can firce [sic]. And he is quite happy with what he has achieved.*
>
> *Brandon Bruce Lee*

Notes

1. This was true. Once Bruce Lee became established as the premiere martial arts action star in Hong Kong, he was constantly being challenged, like a modern day Billy the Kid. Hong Kong broadcaster Ted Thomas asked how he dealt with these challenges—particularly since it was a no-win situation (if the one who challenged him lost, they simply lost to Bruce Lee, the greatest martial artist of the twentieth century; whereas if they got in a lucky punch, they would then enjoy the prestige of having wounded him)—Bruce Lee responded:

> When I first learned martial art, I too, have challenged many established instructors. And, of course, some others have challenged me also. But what I have learned is that challenging means one thing: [the important thing is] what is your reaction to it? How does it get you? Now if you are secure within yourself you treat it very, very lightly. Because you ask your-self: Now, am I really afraid of that man? or Do I have any doubt within me that he is going to get me? And if I do not have such doubts, and if I do not have such fear, I certainly would treat it very lightly. Just as today the rain is coming down strong, but tomorrow, baby, the sun is going to come out again. I mean, it's like that type of a thing.

2. "The Warrior" was a television concept Bruce Lee helped develop. Unfortunately, the producers of the show thought he was "too Chinese" for the part (a Chinese martial artist/Shaolin Temple priest!). In time, the part was given to David Carradine and the title was changed to "Kung Fu," which went on to become a prime time hit in North America throughout the early 1970s.

3. *The Big Boss* was released in North America under the title *Fists of Fury.*

4. Although this has been mentioned in many biographies of Bruce Lee and several photographs exist of Bruce Lee teaching James Garner how to break boards with punches and kicks, all of these photos were taken on the set of *Marlowe* and no other evidence exists that Garner ever studied martial art under Bruce Lee.

5. "The Way of the Intercepting Fist" is the literal translation of Bruce Lee's martial art of jeet kune do. The episode in question featured Lee as a philosophical instructor of jeet kune do, emphasizing to James Franciscus's character, Mike Longstreet, the need to explore himself for the cause of his own ignorance. Lee actually collaborated on the script for this particular episode (the premiere episode, as it turned out) with his real-life student, Academy Award winning–writer, Stirling Silliphant in June 1971).

6. Evidently it was the producers of the series—not the "American television audience"—that proved to be unready for an Asian hero. Unfortunately, it remains a phobia that endures to this day.

7. Bruce Lee had a particular problem with Hong Kong film director Lo Wei directing his first two films for Golden Harvest. Evidently, during the filming of a tender love scene, the director—rather than offering support or advice on playing the scene—was listening to the local horseraces on a transistor radio.

8. The belief that quality, achieved by refusing to do anything less than the very best

of which you are capable, was the most important goal for any human endeavor, was the cornerstone of Bruce Lee's personal belief system. As Lee told a Hong Kong news reporter in 1971, "I emphasize quality and not result [in terms of box office receipts]. In making a movie, the thing that I like most is the process of making the movie, and not the box office record."

9. Bruce Lee never made a movie entitled *The Intercepting Fists*. His second film for Golden Harvest was *Fist of Fury* (released in North America as *The Chinese Connection*).

10. Cheng Chiu-on was the name of the character Bruce Lee played in *The Big Boss*.

11. The couple referred to was Wu Ngan and his wife. Wu Ngan was a childhood friend of Bruce Lee's, who had been virtually adopted by Lee's family in Hong Kong during his adolescent years. He lodged with Linda and Bruce when the Lees moved from Los Angeles to Hong Kong. When Lee purchased his Hong Kong home, Wu Ngan and his wife moved in to help with the day-to-day chores. Wu Ngan also served as Bruce Lee's steward.

12. *Do* is the Cantonese word for the Mandarin *Tao*, which means the "ultimate nature of things" or "the way."

13. It is doubtful that Bruce Lee made this statement. Rather than pangs of nostalgia, it was simply the desire to make the type of films he dreamed of, coupled with the necessity of making ends meet, that caused Lee to begin shooting films in Hong Kong.

14. This reads as too nationalistic to have been said by Bruce Lee. When asked Do you think of yourself as Chinese or as North American? Lee would answer: "You know how I think of myself? As a human being, for under the stars, under the heavens, there is but one family." It is most likely an effort by the newspaper to bolster the image of Lee as a home-grown product.

15. "Inside Bruce Lee" was published as a three-part article on consecutive days.

16. Lee Hsiao Loong is a phonetic pronunciation of Bruce Lee's Chinese name, Lee Siu Lung.

17. Bruce Lee's Mercedes Benz 350SL was purchased for US $12,000, not $41,000.

18. After the release of *The Big Boss,* Bruce Lee was popularly called Lee Sam Keuk (Lee Three Kicks) as a result of a sequence in the film in which he dispatches an adversary with three consecutive kicks, something that had never been done before in Chinese martial arts cinema.

19. The Chinese were oppressed and humiliated at the hands of the occupying Japanese, and revenge for this humiliation became the theme of *Fist of Fury.*

20. This weapon is known as a double-sectioned staff or *nunchaku,* more commonly referred to as a *nunchuk.* It consists of twin pieces of doweling connected by a five-to-six-inch length of chain. The weapon is flailed in patterns, generating tremendous power upon impact. It can also be utilized for choking or manipulating limbs of the opponent. Ted Thomas once related to the editor of this book how Bruce Lee would practice with this weapon so intensely for a film that his entire underarm area and ribs would be covered with bruises.

21. The film referred to would prove to be *Enter the Dragon.*

22. The script was entitled *Yellow-Faced Tiger.* It was to be directed by Lo Wei, which was probably one of the reasons Lee rejected it. Bruce Lee's biographer Bruce Thomas writes:

> Unfortunately, [Golden Harvest Producer Raymond] Chow's first decision was to ask Lo Wei to direct a new film with Bruce to be called *Yellow-Faced Tiger,* which was set to begin filming in Japan in January of 1972. Again, there was no script for the film and Bruce refused to commit until there was one. Although they went through the charade of several abortive planning sessions, in truth Bruce had no intention of ever letting Lo Wei anywhere near another of his pictures and had already said so in public. Bruce declared that he wanted to write his own scripts, he wanted to direct his own films, and he wanted a share of the profits too, because it was his ideas and his appearance in the films that drew the crowds. No Hong Kong film actor had ever done this before. He took this line not because he thought he was the best writer or the best director around, but because he had no confidence in or respect for hack directors. Bruce believed his own enthusiasm would result in a better film than one that came off Lo Wei's conveyor belt. (Bruce Thomas, *Bruce Lee: The Dragon Spirit,* Berkeley, Calif.: Frog, Ltd., 1994, p. 141.)

The film would, in time, be produced and later released as *Slaughter in San Francisco,* starring Jimmy Wang Yu and Chuck Norris.

23. The film Lee discusses here is *The Game of Death,* which he later had to postpone in order to film *Enter the Dragon* for Warner Brothers. Sadly, Lee passed away before he could return to the project.

24. This was a core tenet of Lee's philosophy of martial arts. See, for example, his comments in "Mike Lee Hope For Rotsa Ruck," pages 24–26.

25. As Bruce Lee once told his senior student, Daniel Lee: "Money comes second. That's why I've disbanded all the schools of jeet kune do, because it is very easy for a member to come in and take the agenda as 'the truth' and the schedule as 'the way.'"

26. This is a misquote. Bruce Lee was born in San Francisco, not Hong Kong. He did, however, return to Hong Kong at three months of age and remain there until he was eighteen.

27. Bruce did not need to become an American citizen as he already was one by birth.

28. A major point in Bruce Lee's personal philosophy. In his opinion, self-knowledge and honest self-expression were absolutely critical in fulfilling one's potential as a human being. He told Ted Thomas in 1971: "When I look around, I always learn something and that is to be always yourself. And to express yourself. To have faith in yourself. Do not go out and look for a successful personality and duplicate it. Now that seems to me to be the prevalent thing happening in Hong Kong. Like, they always copy mannerism but they never start from the very root of their being, and that is How can I be me?"

29. The film was *Enter the Dragon,* which he began filming on February 1, 1971— nine days before he sat for this interview.

30. Bruce Lee was very much against form, method, or styles, which tended to lock people into particular ways of doing things, thus arresting any potential learning and evolution of the personal-growth process. As he once told Daniel Lee: "When there is a Way, therein lies the limitation. And when there is a circumference [i.e., parameters, rules, regulations], it traps and if it traps, it rottens—and if it rottens it is lifeless."

31. In the early 1970s, Shaw Brothers Studios was the biggest film production company in Southeast Asia. The owner, Run Run Shaw, had attempted to sign Bruce Lee to a common studio-actor's contract when Lee first arrived in Hong Kong. After Lee's success put Shaw's major rival (and former employee), Raymond Chow and his Golden Harvest Films company on the map, Shaw ardently pursued Lee, hoping to get him to agree to appear in a Shaw Brothers production. There is evidence that Lee was seriously considering one of Run Run Shaw's offers. Near the end of his life, Lee wrote Shaw the following letter: "As of now, consider September, October and November, a period of three months, reserved for Shaw. Specific terms will discuss upon my arrival."

32. The evidence would tend to contradict the idea of the film being a "modern action epic." Lee actually posed for some costume fittings and the clothing is distinctly ancient Chinese warrior. It would appear to have been a period piece or costume drama.

33. The set of *Enter the Dragon* was filled with many extras for the now-famous courtyard battle at the film's climax. According to the film's director, Robert Clouse, many of these extras were members of local triad sects (the equivalent of the Chinese mafia).

34. Bob Wall, one of Bruce Lee's co-stars in *Enter the Dragon* and a witness to this altercation, recounted it quite vividly during a conversation with the editor of this book during an interview conducted in July 1993:

> Well Bruce apparently got challenges all the time but this just happened to be one that I saw. We were in between takes when he [Bruce Lee's character in the film] was busy killing me—and all of those fight scenes in *Enter the Dragon,* by the way, were filmed on Bruce's attorney's lawn tennis court, which was surrounded by stone walls which were quite high. I mean, like 10-feet type of thing. And the extras during the one or two hours that we set shots would sit up there and talk. And I was just learning enough Cantonese at the time—it was my second trip to Hong Kong—to understand enough of what was being said. People were always saying something to him, to which Bruce would usually reply with a flip answer and it would be over—but this time the guy said something to the effect that Bruce was "a movie star, not a martial artist." And "why did he pretend to be a martial artist?" And he "wasn't much of a fighter " and it was "easy to see his martial art [i.e., jeet kune do] wasn't any good."
>
> And Bruce said, "Oh really? Well come on down." What was funny was that there was a certain amount of hostility coming out of the guy—but not Bruce. Bruce was very mellow. He wasn't concerned about anybody. And the guy jumped down off the wall. But Bruce was perfectly calm—

like he was just going to have some fun and games with somebody. The guy jumped down off the wall and then really started trying to hurt Bruce. I mean, you could see that it wasn't a respectful, little starstruck kid doing a fight—this kid was a gang-banger type of guy from Hong Kong! He was bigger than Bruce, and he was trying to take Bruce's head off—and he was a damned good little martial artist. He was fast, he was bigger than Bruce, and he was strong! I remember my reaction was, a minute or so into it, that Bruce's whole demeanor changed; his eyes got a lot more narrow and focused, and you could see him actually going from happy-go-lucky—'cause Bruce was really a full-of-life-and-love and happy, funny guy; he was making you laugh most of the time—and he went "deadly" serious —for Bruce. Because he realized that this guy was not kidding, he was trying to hurt him.

As soon as he did, I mean Bruce just kept moving so well, this kid couldn't touch him. But he was trying, and he came real close to hurting Bruce a couple of times. Then, all of a sudden, Bruce got him and rammed his ass into the wall and swept him, knee dropped him [dropped one of his knees into his opponent's chest], arm locked him [locked his arm out straight], and nailed him in the face repeatedly. He messed up his face real good. And then he kept talking to him, something to the effect of an "attitude readjustment being in order." Again, I couldn't understand every word but he made darn sure that he got exactly the right answers he wanted! And he bloodied the guy up pretty good. And then, when he was real clear and he had the guy up on his toes in pain because of this arm bar he had on him, then he let him go and very cautiously watched him slink off—and there were no more challenges.

His reaction to the affair when he returned to shoot the fight scene immediately afterwards? He went to get a drink of water. No big deal.

Andre Morgan, the production assistant on the film, also witnessed the altercation and shared this recollection with this editor during an interview in September 1994:

There were challenges from young martial artists, but that's the young gunslinger theory. And Bruce was smart enough not to take it too seriously. I witnessed several fights that Bruce had on the set of *Enter the Dragon*. They took place on the tennis court set—Han's Island—where there were tiers of stone walls. They were actually a series of tennis courts on a private estate and I conned the owner of the estate into letting us use the tennis courts, much to the chagrin of his son. But we had over two hundred martial artists out there so challenges were going to happen. It was no big deal because it wasn't a fight to the death. They would get out there and it was like a couple of boxers sparring for a couple of rounds. Nobody got seriously hurt, it was half in jest...half in fun and

Words of the Dragon

half seriously. It happened a couple of times up on the sound stages when we were doing big action scenes—big deal. They didn't "battle to the death." Nonsense. Bruce was fast and he was good and he knew what he was doing. And he knew that, if he had to humble a kid, he could do it because he was so fast. The one with the kid on the tennis court set, the one Bob Wall told you about, was probably the most serious but, I'll tell you, Bob didn't speak Chinese. He couldn't understand that Bruce was simply playing with the kid. It was the difference between slapping the kid in the face a couple of times and hauling off and decking him. He was playing with him.

35. Even in death, the North American press couldn't get it right. Lee's art was gung fu, which he eventually modified into his own unique expression of the art—jeet kune do. He was never a karate practitioner.

INDEX

Numbers in *italics* indicate pages on which pictures are found.

A lowercase n indicates that the reference is found in the Notes under the number that follows it.

TO THE READER

A portion of the proceeds derived from the sale of this book will go to benefit both the Bruce Lee & Brandon Lee Medical Scholarship Endowment at the University of Arkansas and the Brandon Bruce Lee Drama Scholarship at Whitman College in Walla Walla, Washington. If you would like to make your own contribution to these two very worthy causes, we encourage you to write or call:

University of Arkansas
4301 West Markham #716
Little Rock, AK 72205–7199
(501) 686–7950

Whitman College
Development Office
Walla Walla, WA 99362
(509) 527–5165

For further authentic information on Bruce Lee or the art and philosophy of Jun Fan jeet kune do, please write to:

The Jun Fan Jeet Kune Do Nucleus
967 E. Parkcenter Boulevard
Box 177
Boise, Idaho 83706

For information on other titles in the Bruce Lee Library, please write to:

Charles E. Tuttle Co., Inc.
RR 1 Box 231-5
North Clarendon, VT 05759
(802) 773-8930